Praise for

THE WAL★MART WAY

by Don Soderquist

"This fascinating story of the American Dream has become a part of the Americana—vision, discipline, passion, when governed by conscience, changes the world. The centerpiece is people. Read this book and enjoy the ride!"

–Dr. Stephen R. Covey | Author, *The 7 Habits of Highly Effective People* and *The 8th Habit: From Effectiveness to Greatness*

★

"The Wal-Mart Way is a fascinating and historic look at the story of one of the world's most legendary companies, written from the inside by Sam Walton's long-time friend and confidante. You'll learn a lot about how a great company was built."

–Jack Welch | Former Chairman and CEO, General Electric

★

"Retailing has always been in my blood. Like Sam Walton, I spent as much time as I could visiting other people's stores, but through the years I learned that Wal-Mart is in a class all by itself. It's the epitome of retail. The story of this unbelievable organization began in—of all places—Bentonville, Arkansas, and is the greatest retail story of all times. Don Soderquist gives us insight on how it was accomplished and offers a useful guide to entrepreneurs everywhere who want to take advantage of our great free enterprise system. *The Wal-Mart Way* truly shows what can be achieved out of this life. Great reading."

–Bernie Marcus | Cofounder, The Home Depot

"Sam Walton was a passionate man. His passions were his God, his family, his country, and his business. All of us who knew Sam Walton have wished we could leave for posterity a proper portrait of this uncommon man. One of his closest friends and business associates has done it. In *The Wal-Mart Way* you are going to meet Mister Sam through the friendly eyes of Don Soderquist. Good for you."

–Paul Harvey | Paul Harvey News

"As Don Soderquist can uniquely relate, the Wal-Mart phenomenon is the result of a strong culture and clear values, sound strategy and vision, outstanding leadership, and disciplined management execution—necessary ingredients to any great organization's success."

–Frederick W. Smith | Founder and CEO, FedEx Corporation

"I always hoped that Don Soderquist would take the time to explain the foundations of Wal-Mart's success. He has done it superbly, capturing its essence—from Sam Walton's vision that started it all; to the unrelenting focus on the customer; to respect for people and values, teamwork, and relationships; to the never-ending quest for improvement and growth and commitment to excellence. Soderquist has done this in a way that not only explains Wal-Mart but can be applied to any institution, profit or nonprofit. The lessons in *The Wal-Mart Way* are at once concrete, accessible, highly engaging, and broadly applicable. This is a book that countless readers will benefit from."

–John E. Pepper Jr. | Retired Chairman and CEO, Procter & Gamble

★

"Although many books and stories have been published featuring Sam Walton and the amazing success of his company, no one relates the inside story of the company better than Don Soderquist. Sam Walton was . . . visionary, an inspiring motivator, and an extremely intelligent individual with high personal integrity . . . His remarkable ability to blend strategies, operating principles and personal values together formed a company culture that carried the organization to unparalleled success . . . Above all, the Wal-Mart success story is an exciting and encouraging example of the unlimited opportunities available in the American free enterprise system. *The Wal-Mart Way* is a book that readers will find openly revealing, highly informative and truly enlightening."

–Stanley C. Gault | Retired Chairman and CEO, Goodyear Tire & Rubber Company, Rubbermaid, Inc.

★

"Don Soderquist has written a book that not only gives us insight into the success of Wal-Mart, but also shows us how we can be responsible role models in our own businesses and communities. Thank you, Don, for clearly defining the how-to's of being an ethical leader in the 21st century."

–Anne Beiler | Founder and CEO, Auntie Anne's, Inc.

★

"*The Wal-Mart Way* terrifically captures the Wal-Mart soul in a way only Don Soderquist could do. A powerful story of the past and a roadmap for the future, it is presented in a very engaging way."

–Steven S. Reinemund | Chairman and CEO, PepsiCo

★

"This is a story about the vision, values, drive, and commitment that created the strongest retail machine ever. It's about compassion, caring, and understanding. It is not a history story; it is the story of how it all gets done. It's *The Wal-Mart Way*—envied, emulated, and often feared. And it is eloquently told by one of the key architects of the culture that created it all."

–Joe Scarlett | Chairman of the Board, Tractor Supply Company

THE
WAL★MART®
WAY

THE
WAL★MART®
WAY

THE INSIDE STORY OF THE SUCCESS OF THE WORLD'S LARGEST COMPANY

DISCARD

Don Soderquist

NELSON BUSINESS
A Division of Thomas Nelson Publishers
Since 1798

www.thomasnelson.com

Published in Nashville, Tennessee, by Thomas Nelson, Inc.

Nelson Books titles may be purchased in bulk for educational, business, fund-raising, or sales
promotional use. For information, please e-mail: SpecialMarkets@ThomasNelson.com.

All Scripture quotations, unless otherwise indicated, are taken from the HOLY BIBLE:
NEW INTERNATIONAL VERSION®. Copyright © 1973, 1978, 1984 by International Bible
Society. Used by permission of Zondervan Publishing House. All rights reserved.

Scripture marked NLT is taken from the *Holy Bible*, New Living Translation, copyright ©
1996. Used by permission of Tyndale House Publishers, Inc., Wheaton, Illinois 60189.
All rights reserved.

Cover Photo by Debrorah Billingsley Photography

Library of Congress Cataloging-in-Publication Data

Soderquist, Don.
  The Wal-Mart way: the inside story of the success of the world's largest company / Don
Soderquist.
    p. cm.
  Includes bibliographical references.
  ISBN 0-7852-6119-2 (hardcover)
  1. Wal-Mart (Firm)—Management. 2. Discount houses (Retail trade)—United
    States—Management. I. Title.
  HF5429.215.U6S63 2005
  381'.14906573--dc22

                              2004028644

Printed in the United States of America
05 06 07 08 09—5 4 3 2 1

★★★

This book is dedicated to Sam Walton, in memory,
and the hundreds of thousands of Wal-Mart associates who
helped make this remarkable story a reality.

Contents

Preface   xiii

Introduction   *The Wal-Mart Way*   xv

Chapter 1   Growing Dreams   1

Chapter 2   Vision—The Power of
                   Seeing What Others Don't See   11

Chapter 3   The Power of Culture   25

Chapter 4   People Make the Difference   49

Chapter 5   The Customer Is the Boss   81

Chapter 6   A Passion for Excellence   103

Chapter 7   The Execution Imperative   117

Chapter 8   Technology—the Ultimate
                   Change Agent   137

Chapter 9   Reinventing the Supply Chain   151

Chapter 10   Creating Supplier Relationships   165

Chapter 11   Never Stop Growing   177

Chapter 12   Good Neighbors   185

Conclusion   Scaling New Heights   201

About the Author   205

Acknowledgments   207

Appendix A: The Wal-Mart Way Principles   209

Appendix B: Perspective on External Criticism
                    of Wal-Mart   211

Recommended Reading   213

Notes   215

PREFACE

It's what you learn after you know it all that counts.
—John Wooden

The shelves of bookstores are filled with many fine books on leadership and business success. Why another one? I believe there is always a need for simple truths—no matter how often they are told.

The Wal-Mart story is full of simple but important truths. It is a story that has mystified some, frustrated others, and been admired by many. It is a story about principled, focused leadership that has been able to effectively and consistently balance values and the bottom line in a way that has seldom occurred. It is a story about the power of the free-enterprise system and how that system is the engine that drives democracy. It is a story about trust—the basis of all successful relationships. It is a story about a special man, a special group of people, and a special organization. It is, I truly believe, a story that has positive applications for millions of people and organizations.

This book is not intended to be a history of Wal-Mart. It is not written to tell about the wonderful things the company has or has not done, though even the most casual reader will quickly understand how strongly I believe in the Wal-Mart way of doing business.

The two reasons I decided to write a book are both related to helping others. First, for all Wal-Mart associates, past, present, and future, this is a means of learning, celebrating, strengthening, and preserving the unique culture of our company. Second, and equally important, this is a way of sharing principles of success with others—small-business owners, high school and college students, leaders of Fortune 500 companies, middle managers, entrepreneurs, and countless others—who may learn from our experiences and gain inspiration and insights to fuel growth in their personal lives and in all their endeavors.

If, by reading this book, a person can say, "Ah-ha, now I get it; I see something that could really help me," then my purpose as an author has been fulfilled. One of the great motivators in my own life is to see someone who has been dealing with a particular issue experience authentic life change. Nothing compares to seeing the light go on in the eyes of someone who is experiencing a major breakthrough in life.

I recognize that we live in a critical and somewhat skeptical age. I understand that some readers will open this book with a predisposition to resist the ideas of the Wal-Mart Way. I understand that and, in fact, I enjoy a lively and spirited discussion. I would just note that there is a certain irony about breakthroughs: they frequently come in very different ways than we might expect and for reasons that we don't even realize. They are often surprising and they can be dynamite! Breakthroughs are most of all about self-discovery. I encourage all readers to engage the following pages with a spirit of openness. The Chinese proverb is true: when the student is ready, the teacher appears.

If I can help someone understand and apply concepts of success that he or she otherwise would have missed, then writing this book will have been one of the most rewarding experiences of my life.

Don Soderquist

THE WAL-MART WAY

There are no secrets to success. It is the result of preparation,
hard work, learning from failure.

—*General Colin Powell*

Most observers of the business world would acknowledge that the Wal-Mart story is an amazing story of success and is a great example—maybe the greatest example—of the free-enterprise system at work. How a man and his wife could invest six thousand dollars of personal savings and money borrowed from family members into a small business that fifty-five years later would become the largest company in the world is nothing short of remarkable, if not miraculous.

The Wal-Mart story begins with a man and his dream, supported by his convictions of right and wrong. The story begins to take shape with his uncanny ability to inspire a group of people to embrace his vision and create not only a one-of-a-kind company but a revolutionary business model that impacted the standard of living for millions upon millions of everyday people in America and worldwide. The story gains momentum as it is played out by humble men and women who were able to aim well beyond the horizon of the status quo, and who are still dreaming big dreams today.

The story continues to be written. It could, in fact, be duplicated by many others, and yet it is possible that it will never be written again.

So What's the Secret?

Frequently, I'm asked the question, "How has Wal-Mart done it?" or "What's the secret?" I must humbly confess that there is no secret, no magic formula. The story is not a complicated novel with a cast of thousands and numerous subplots to follow. It is possibly so simple that unless you read it with discernment and an open heart, you may miss its significance. Sometimes the simplest truths are the hardest to grasp because they seem so obvious. Many bright, educated, articulate people are turned off by simplicity, thinking, *It can't be that easy, or other people would have done it. Where's the real magic?* Others dismiss the story as sheer luck. Sam was just in the right place at the right time.

If vision, hard work, integrity, focus on the customer, passion for excellence, and having fun at work is luck, then we, indeed, were some of the luckiest people alive.

I don't want to suggest for one minute that it was easy—it wasn't. And it certainly wasn't simply being fortunate—though most of us feel incredibly blessed to be a part of the story. What brought us to where we are is a lot of hard work by a lot of wonderful, dedicated people over the years. There were many tough decisions and many obstacles to overcome, and our journey in the business world has been far from risk-free; but had it been easy, the accomplishment would not have been as great and would not have tasted so sweet.

How Then Did We Do It?

No single factor led us to success—a number of things that we did combined to create a synergy that multiplied the impact and compounded the results of our efforts. If you look at any business or organization that has grown and achieved substantial success over the long term, you'll notice several key factors that made a big difference. I believe that Wal-Mart has a special story to tell, that there are several distinctive and unique factors that played a major role in our success. Here is a preview of what I'll cover through stories and personal reflections in the following chapters:

1. Wal-Mart began with the dream of one man, Sam Walton, to own his own store. He cherished and nurtured that dream in such a way—with a sense of sacred duty and a willingness to let the dream enable him to grow personally—that the dream itself grew into something beyond his or anyone else's wildest imagination.

2. Wal-Mart was built on (and maintains) an exciting vision of what we could become, which was not based on financial goals, but on

serving others. No matter what the challenge or decision in front of us, we refused to depart from that vision. Of course, we developed a product and the necessary strategies, resources, and people to reach a profit model that would lead to long-term success. Every truly successful organization strives for sustainability. But even as we sought to be a financially viable company, we never swerved from our original vision of serving our customers.

3. Wal-Mart created and has sustained a unique company culture based on core values and beliefs that have been woven into the very fabric of the company. Ask the Wal-Mart associates who have been with the company twenty, thirty, forty years and longer, and they'll con-

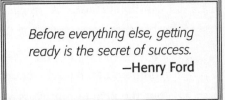

Before everything else, getting ready is the secret of success.
—Henry Ford

vince you that the fundamental culture has not changed with growth or time. In my judgment, the single most important element in the continued, remarkable success of Wal-Mart is our culture. I think you'll find our plan for sharing culture with each successive generation of leadership to be profound.

4. Wal-Mart demonstrates a genuine commitment to our associates. This shows up in competitive salaries, investment options, benefits, a promote-from-within philosophy, and in other ways. But I think what truly stands out is the amazingly open interaction between the various levels of responsibility. Everyone is treated with respect and dignity. It is a core belief that every associate is vital to the success of the company, which is why so many of our best ideas and practices have been forged in the front lines of our stores.

5. Wal-Mart emphasizes and reinforces with all associates that they must have a burning focus to satisfy every single customer every day. We all recognize that the customers are the reason we are in business and that it is our responsibility to do our best to exceed

their expectations, whether it be a friendly greeter at the front door, all merchandise in stock, or our everyday low-pricing strategy.

6. Wal-Mart encourages a passion for excellence in every area of our business. We are always striving to get better and to be the best that we can be. As a result, we are not afraid to change and, in fact, we embrace change proactively. We don't wait for major problems to arise but attempt to make improvements to systems and dynamics that are already working comparatively well.

7. Wal-Mart thrives on execution, on making things happen, on a can-do attitude. This means getting the job done and achieving objectives with record speed and accuracy. It means guarding against an increasingly complex and self-serving bureaucracy. A company can have a wonderful vision and an excellent product, but the people must execute for that vision and product to go anywhere. In that same regard, we believe that everything we do should be done with a sense of urgency—no delays, no excuses, no red tape—do it now! As part of our determination to execute well, we pay close attention to details at all levels. We believe that even when a person is promoted or becomes an officer of the company, he or she still has a responsibility to stay appropriately involved in the frontline details of our business.

8. From the very beginning, Wal-Mart invested and continues to invest significant capital in the practical application of technology. Many companies have made enormous expenditures in the area of technology, with poor returns. The key to achieving strong returns on investment is to tie all system development and implementation into your most vital business functions. For Wal-Mart, that kept technology focused on customer satisfaction, which has in turn made technological prowess a key competitive advantage for Wal-Mart.

9. Wal-Mart's quest for excellence kept us working on the most

basic operations in our business. The simple act of getting our merchandise from the supplier's dock to the store shelf received numerous makeovers, and we made an art of stripping excess cost and waste of any kind from our logistics operations. We ended up revolutionizing supply-chain management for the entire retail industry.

10. Wal-Mart fostered relationships with suppliers based on openness and trust—again, revolutionizing the way business is done in an entire industry. Every business enterprise involves relationships, whether they are among your own associates, your customers, your suppliers, your board of directors, your shareholders, or your communities. We believe that these relationships must be maintained at the highest level of honesty and candor at all times. Trust relationships ultimately are the basis of any long-term loyalty and create a climate of success for all parties.

11. Wal-Mart implemented a carefully thought-out and tenacious growth strategy, plowing a large percentage of profits back into the company to aggressively expand into new markets and to equally aggressively revitalize existing stores, clubs, and distribution centers.

12. Wal-Mart made an early commitment to corporate responsibility. We still believe that it is important to invest back into the communities we serve and into the lives of our customers. We have never done it out of a sense of obligation or in order to get publicity for what we do, but rather because we believed it was the right thing to do and wanted to be instrumental in the growth, well-being, and prosperity of our communities.

As icing on the cake, we not only worked hard—but we had a lot of fun doing it. We never saw the dynamics of work and fun as incompatible. If you're going to spend a large percentage of your waking hours at work, why not enjoy it? We kept it informal and comfortable with everyone, joked around a little—often at the expense of senior management—and did all we could to create a fun, upbeat environment that would take the drudgery out of the day-to-day routine and provide a positive atmosphere for everyone.

This, in a nutshell, is the Wal-Mart Way. What do you think so far?

Maybe you're not convinced it is applicable in your organization or company. Maybe you're not yet persuaded that our success was based on a

> *The secret of success in life is for a man to be ready for his opportunity when it comes.*
> —Benjamin Disraeli

carefully crafted set of principles but was more a matter of luck and timing. Maybe you're already completely satisfied with how your organization does things. Maybe you're overwhelmed by a seemingly endless array of challenges and problems in your company. But, just maybe, you are open to testing the waters and learning from one company's experience and story.

Okay, I'll tell you a secret after all. The principles I share with you in the following pages will dramatically work for you too. I know firsthand, because I was there!

In 1980, I joined Wal-Mart Stores, Inc., as executive vice president and served in several other executive positions until my appointment in early 1988 to vice chairman and chief operating officer. In January 1999 I was promoted to senior vice chairman of the corporation.

For Reflection and Action:

1. What factors would you say have been most instrumental in your organization's successes? Your personal success?

2. What new attitudes and actions do you need to adopt to make your business more successful?

3. Finish this sentence: The one thing that I most hope to get out of reading this book is . . .

Chapter 1

Growing Dreams

The uncommon man is merely the common man thinking and
dreaming of success in larger terms and in more fruitful areas.
　　　　　　　　　　　　　　　　　　　　—Melvin Powers

Wal-Mart Way Principle #1

Every successful venture begins with a dream that requires determination,
passion, and the willingness to grow if it is to be fulfilled.

Once upon a time there was a man, and that man had a dream. In some ways it was an ordinary dream, not so different from the dreams of millions of others. But it was also uncommon as dreams go. It wasn't to build the tallest building in the world or to build the longest bridge. It wasn't to make a million dollars before he was thirty years old, or to become the richest man in the world. It wasn't to bring honor and glory to himself, or to be one of the most recognized men in the world. Nor was it to be the president of the country he loved so much. His dream was really quite simple: he wanted to own his own store.

Well, maybe his dream wasn't quite that simple. Because he had some very firm ideas on why—and how—he wanted to own a store. His dream was empowered by his desire to:

- Serve people well.
- Build a winning team.
- Work hard.
- Impact people's lives for good.
- Have fun.
- Support his family.
- Honor his Lord.

But what made this man's dream extraordinary—and grow beyond his or anyone else's wildest expectations—was that he cultivated it with a personal commitment to learn, to grow, to accomplish in one lifetime all that he could. One day at a time and every day.

That man's name was Sam Walton, and so the dream began.

- He bought his own store—a small variety store.
- He found a supplier of merchandise—Ben Franklin.
- He worked really, really hard.
- He had fun and created excitement wherever he went.
- He touched people's lives.
- He treated people well.
- He made many friends.
- He was a loving husband and father.
- His sales increased, and his profits grew.

The First Detour—All Roads Lead to Bentonville

Sam unexpectedly lost the lease on his first store in Newport, Arkansas. Did that end the dream? Not on your life; he had tasted success, and it tasted good. He had the fever now and more than ever, he knew he could do it—he knew it could be done!

So the dream continued. He searched the countryside, found a town named Bentonville, Arkansas, and pinpointed a new store location. He improved his business methods by constantly talking to his associates, his competitors, and his customers. When things didn't work, he changed them. When customers asked for more value and variety, he worked doggedly to fulfill those requests. He did a lot of things right. (And, of course, he made a few mistakes along the way.) And with a growing passion for his dream, with a smile and homespun charisma, he created a buzz, an excitement, a sense of anticipation around and within his company. He had a lot of fun doing it. And his sales continued to grow.

Sam was always looking to the future and his dream. Why not two stores? Why not three—or even four? He went to his brother and said, "Bud, I need your help. It's getting too big for me. This business I have going really works. If you treat people special and you sell customers what they want to buy, they keep coming back. But I need to make some changes if I want to grow. I can't keep up with all the tasks and all the details anymore. I'll stay involved, you can bet on that, but I can't do it all myself. I need to start depending a whole lot more on others.

"Please come and join me. Let's find some good people. Let's train them. Let's show them what we want them to do. Let's trust them with running our stores, and then let's pay them what they earn from the profits of our stores. Let's talk to our customers and our associates. We need to keep getting better. We need to learn from our competitors but do it even better than they do. We need to change the shelves in the store, the merchandise we sell, the signs, and the store hours. We've got to do whatever it takes to satisfy our customers."

A Second Detour—the Birth of Wal-Mart

Sam's business continued to grow. He and his brother, Bud, continued to add stores until by 1962 they had built a regional chain of fifteen stores. They had become Ben Franklin's largest franchisee.

But not content to rest on his already considerable accomplishments, Sam traveled across the land and watched what his most successful competitors were doing. They were building larger and larger stores.

"Our stores are too small," he said to Bud. "There's not enough room for all the merchandise our customers are asking for. They don't want to have to drive to larger cities to buy the merchandise they need and want right now. They also want the lower prices that they pay in the larger cities. We've got to rework our plan and start building bigger stores if we want to satisfy our customers."

The man needed to change and grow along with his dream to get where he wanted to go, and he asked for help.

"Mr. Ben Franklin Company," Sam said, "please help me build larger stores in my small towns. I know it's not been done before, but my people are asking for more assortments and lower prices. I've got an idea for them. Will you work with me and franchise these larger stores? Will you sell the merchandise to me at a lower price since I need to reduce the prices to my customers? You'll do okay, too, because I'll be buying a lot more merchandise from you."

"It will never work," they said. "We can't do that. There are not enough people out there for discount stores. You will never be able to generate enough business in those small towns. Larger stores work in the larger cities. Smaller stores for smaller towns. Everyone knows that. Be content. You're already the biggest and best at what you do. And by the way, we can't sell the merchandise to you for a lower price than we sell it to everyone else. The risk in this plan is too great for everyone—including you."

"I'll gladly be your guinea pig," Sam argued. "Let me take the risk. This is something I've got to try."

"Sorry, but no," was their final answer. "You've done a great job, Sam Walton, and we respect what you have accomplished, but we're not going in that direction."

"Then we'll have to do it on our own," he said to Bud. He knew change was necessary to follow his dream—a simple dream that had stayed true to its ideals—and he wasn't going to give up now.

Wal-Mart was born.

The Dream Continues to Grow

Not giving up meant that Sam had to acquire computers, warehouses, trucks, and many other things that were all brand-new to his business. It also meant the birth of Wal-Mart discount stores. It was a big risk, it took a lot of courage and openness to change, but he and his associates made it work. Little by little, the dream would grow one successful Wal-Mart at a time.

In early 1971, Sam wrote to all Wal-Mart associates and said:

If any generalization is true of retailing in the 70s, it would have to be that our business is one of constant change. Increasingly, this is just as true in our small trade centers as well as in the larger metropolitan areas. Consequently, it is most important that all of us in Wal-Mart be alert and curious to new trends and developments in retailing. It is imperative that each new process be studied and analyzed thoroughly to see if we can adopt the idea for Wal-

Mart, but the total key for our stores is that we retain our philosophy of being not only the dominant store in our areas, but more importantly, that we do the best job of anybody around in rendering effective, friendly customer service.

Sam continued to be involved in the stores, with his people, in his community, and in his church. He remained a common man, always giving credit to others for everything he achieved. But he refused to be complacent—he was always challenging, always thinking, always experimenting, always raising the bar, and always striving for the impossible.

Our goals and achievements for 1971 have all been met and exceeded as of this date. Most people and other companies would have said that what we have done is impossible. I'm convinced that nothing is impossible for this Wal-Mart team and that we'll again meet these goals and challenges as projected for 1972. This can be done. Again, let me thank each of you for what you have done to make 1971 our biggest and best year yet. I'm confident 1972 will be even better. Together we can do it.

He continued to be the leader and servant, the student and teacher, the preacher and critic, the coach and cheerleader.

We have quite a company. As I stated this week in New York, it is one composed of exceptionally interested, enthused, and dedicated people all determined to achieve our Wal-Mart program, and make it totally the best retail chain in the United States. More and more our long range sales goal of one billion dollars by 1981 looks attainable and entirely likely as we build a broader base, increase competence of all management levels, and create a company and program that is not only interesting and challenging for all of us but also creates good benefits and economic security for all families. Our policy of being fair and honest with each other must continue at every level. Nothing can stop Wal-Mart as we maintain this team spirit, morale, and continue to work together. That is an unbeatable combination. Let's keep the doors open. It will be tough but I'm confident.

The dream kept growing and with that growth came many changes— the stores looked better and better and service to the customers improved as Sam and his team worked to perfect all aspects of operations and merchandising. Change wasn't easy, even for Sam. In change there are always risks. Every organization wants to grow, but there are just as many if not more risks when a company gets bigger. And for a company built on a sense of family, it's possible to lose the personal touch with the people and with the customers as well. Recognizing that, Sam wrote:

> *When people are through changing, they're through.*
> —Bruce Barton

> *Sometimes I wish we were the small company we once were not so long ago, so I could personally see all of you occasionally, and thank you for the good job being done. It's much more difficult now to get around, but it doesn't mean that any of us in management appreciate any of you any less than ten years ago. Our situation is different in 1975 than in 1965. Our company has increased in size over 25 times in ten years with our total personnel increasing from about 250 in 1965 to approximately 6,500 in 1975.*

Yes, the company grew and the better it became, the bigger it got. No matter how big Wal-Mart became, though, Sam shared his dream with all of us one by one, and we all became a part of it. Near the end of his life he wrote to his associates again:

> *I had no vision of the scope of what I would start, but I always had confidence that as long as we did our work well, and were good to our customers, there would be no limits to us. I would like to be remembered as a good friend to everyone whose lives I've touched as their friend, as someone who meant something to them or helped them in some way. That is important. I have such strong feelings for the folks in our company. They have meant so much to me.*

He led us to become the most successful retail company in the United States—and the world. In the end, he did receive honor and glory from the world over, including several U.S. presidents; he did make friends across the land and was recognized by sight and name probably as much as any single man in the United States. So, you see, the dream—to do good for others—resulted in what others often dream about.

If Sam Were Here Today

Now Sam's gone and things have changed, and they will never be the same again. But things changed while he was here, and more than anyone, he was the agent for those changes. Were he here today, his encouragement would be, "Hold fast to what is important, but change what needs to be changed. Change is inevitable—so let's be a positive force in the midst of it." In the words of James Champy, author of *Reengineering Management*:

> *It is not enough for a leader to have a vision. A leader needs to attract followers, men and women who can commit themselves to the new ideal and necessity of customer focus. But if the mobilization process is to succeed those followers must become leaders too, finding their own sense of purpose in the shared challenge and spreading the call and vision of change.*

Sam accomplished great things—he created the Wal-Mart Way—by valuing people and hard work. He made serving people his number-one priority. He asked for help when he needed it. He allowed his coworkers to share in the dream with him, and he told them how valuable they were and how much he appreciated them. He worked hard. He wasn't afraid to change in order to stay ahead of the game.

Growing Dreams by Growing People

Because of Sam's flexibility and tenaciousness, his dream of owning his own store succeeded and grew. And along the way, thousands upon thousands of individuals grew right along with that dream. Here are two remarkable stories of two remarkable Wal-Mart associates who captured the company's vision.

Theresa Barrera

Theresa started working for the Sam's Club in Corpus Christi, Texas, as a part-time cashier in November 1985. Theresa's mother passed away after Theresa had been working at Sam's for only six weeks. She was impressed and touched that two of the club's management team came to the funeral.

In the fall of 1986, she was awarded a Wal-Mart scholarship that enabled her to finish her college education. At approximately the same time, she began working full time in another hourly job.

In January 1990, she was promoted to a management position in the home office as an internal auditor and moved to Bentonville. In 1993, she was promoted to a position as special projects coordinator in the international division. Her next job in that division was as a buyer.

In 1995, she moved into the Wal-Mart stores division as a buyer and was promoted to divisional merchandise manager in 1999. In 2001, she was promoted to vice president of Wal-Mart and today is responsible for more than $5.2 billion of merchandise purchases for Wal-Mart stores.

Theresa shares:

> *I personally feel I have been a very lucky woman. Nineteen years ago I started working at Sam's as a part-time cashier. Never in my wildest dreams did I believe I could achieve what I have. I will tell you I was given a chance. Wal-Mart has challenged me and I worked really hard to prove myself. Not only do I have an amazing career, I have two amazing daughters. There is nothing more satisfying than living the life you want. Wal-Mart encourages all of us to have mentors and "mentees." I feel this is so important so we continue to grow and develop new young talent—just as someone did with me.*

Kevin Turner

In 1986, Kevin joined Wal-Mart as a temporary cashier in a Wal-Mart store in Ada, Oklahoma. He was a student at East Central University and was working his way through college. When he graduated, he decided to become a full-time Wal-Mart associate and was assigned to a position as a company auditor.

After several years in that role, he was promoted to an entry-level job in the technology department. He continued to be promoted into increasingly higher level positions in technology and eventually rose to senior vice president and CIO of Wal-Mart in 1999.

Kevin was always involved in using technology to serve the needs of the business with a keen eye on the needs of the customer. He always demonstrated a great sense of urgency in all that he did. In 2002, Kevin was promoted to president and CEO of Sam's Clubs, a $30 billion division of Wal-Mart.

Kevin comments:

Early on I heard our leaders use the term "cross pollination" and describe how important it was and how big a part it had played in the formulation of Wal-Mart. After my third job in as many divisions within the company, I came to realize how blessed I had been to learn from the variety of experiences and people I had been exposed to, each contributing to my career and preparing me for the next job. Not only does being "cross pollinated" broaden your point of view but it also helps us become a better company by having people who can leverage the entire enterprise in the best way possible.

I believe that leadership skills are transferable and can be taught. Theresa and Kevin are great examples of this. There are literally thousands of stories that are similar to these, and they continue to happen every day in Wal-Mart.

A Special Note to Wal-Mart Associates from Don

"Today the dream is the same—only now it is our dream. Yours and mine. Because of the man who had a dream, we have changed the way we all think, act, and lead. Because of the man who had a dream, the face of retailing has been changed the world over. The way we buy and sell merchandise, the way we ship and store it has changed. Because of the man who had a dream, we have changed the way customers are greeted and satisfied. Because of the man who had a dream, we have changed how people are treated and how businesses are run. And because of the man who had a dream, we will continue to grow and to change what we do and the way we do it."

Wal-Mart Growth by Decade

BY DECADE	TOTAL REVENUE	# OF STORES	# OF ASSOCIATES
1/31/1970	$30.8 million	32	900
1/31/1980	$1.2 billion	276	21,000
1/31/1990	$25.8 billion	1,528	275,000
1/31/2000	$165 billion	3,985	1,140,000
1/31/2004	$256.3 billion	4,906	1,500,000

For Reflection and Action:

1. Have you ever had a dream, whether simple or grand, that you would love to accomplish in your life?

2. What are some "detours" you have experienced in your personal and work life? How have you responded to setbacks and challenges?

3. How comfortable are you with change? Are you flexible? Are you committed to growth?

Chapter 2

Vision—The Power of Seeing What Others Don't See

*Discovery consists of seeing what everybody has seen and thinking
what nobody has thought.*

—Albert von Szent-Gyorgy

Wal-Mart Way Principle #2

You must have a vision that allows you to see a bigger, better, stronger you in
the future—while never taking your eyes off of who you are and
what you are doing today.

Vision is the beginning point of any great endeavor. Christopher
Columbus saw a great continent beyond the western horizon, while
others saw the jagged edge of the world. Roger Bannister pictured himself
crossing the finish line in a one-mile race in less than four minutes, while
others saw only the limits of physical attainment. NASA scientists envisioned a human walking on the moon, while other brilliant minds had
mathematically proven that such space travel was impossible.

Vision is a picture of how we would like tomorrow to look—or, put
another way, how we would like ourselves to look tomorrow. Every good
leadership book identifies vision as an essential characteristic of a leader,
and every good leader has learned his or her responsibility to create and
communicate a vision. But the danger is that talk of vision has become so
prevalent—maybe even so commonplace—that many leaders take the
process and discipline of vision-casting for granted.

How about you? How much time and energy have you given to creating
and sharing a personal and corporate vision?

Sam Walton's Simple Vision

Just as Sam began with a simple dream—to own his own store—his vision would likewise have not been considered very grand, sophisticated, or ambitious by most of his business contemporaries. Even with his vision becoming an enormous and ongoing reality, there are still experts who discount the power of Sam's vision, chalking up the Wal-Mart story to luck rather than the tenacious pursuit of a vision. I would argue that few things are more powerful and dynamic than a vision.

When he looked into the future, Sam didn't see Wal-Mart as the largest

> Warren Buffet estimates that Wal-Mart saves consumers $10 billion annually, primarily through its everyday low prices. In the March 2003 issue of *Fortune* magazine he said:
>
> *You can add it all up and they (Wal-Mart) have contributed to the financial well-being of the American public more than any institution I can think of.*

retailer in the world. He simply wanted to provide a better shopping experience for people living in small towns. He wanted to improve their standard of living by providing quality goods at low prices in a pleasant shopping environment. He wanted to accomplish this with a team of dedicated people . (Sam checked a person's smile before he checked his educational background!) He strongly believed that if his team of associates felt as if they were part of a family, it would make his vision a joy and a success. And ultimately, as a smart businessman, Sam realized that if the stores were successful, he could continue to grow the company and touch more and more customers with his vision.

Notice that Sam did not begin with a vision to create the largest retail chain in the United States—much less found the largest company in the world. Millions of people have ambitious dreams and grand ideas for the future but fail to build the support and enthusiasm of others—investors, customers, their own employees—maybe even themselves. If you want people to follow you, be aware that they will always relate much better and on a much deeper level to something that is worthwhile in and of itself rather than financial objectives.

Sam never articulated a vision of being the biggest and richest. He did have a simple business plan that would make money and that he believed would likewise make the world a better place. And his team embraced the vision.

The customers liked what they saw too. They continued to shop at Wal-Mart, making the vision a reality—and helping it to grow beyond anything Sam ever dreamed of. Sam never wavered in his vision to provide service to small-town America, but as success bred success, he began to test his stores in midsized markets and then in the major metropolitan centers of America.

The vision grew, but the fundamental premise never changed: improve the standard of living for everyday people by providing quality goods at low prices.

The Vision Grows—Sam's Club Is Born

In 1982, David Glass (who was then the CFO and who later became CEO of Wal-Mart), Sam, and I were in Southern California for a retailers' convention, where we met with Sam's good friend Sol Price, an entrepreneurial retailer who had developed a retail-wholesale concept he called the Price Club. It was a warehouse club that required you to buy a membership and pay an annual fee in order to shop there. The primary customers were small-business owners who could buy merchandise at wholesale prices (or lower) and resell to their customers at substantial savings. They could also buy many of their supplies at the Price Club. Individual retail customers could buy memberships and shop there as well.

Though not everyone was optimistic about a business model where people would pay up front to shop in your store, the idea was so unique and intriguing that we decided to visit one of the clubs and see what we could learn. (Sam would never let us get away from the habit of visiting our competitors to learn how we could improve, a trait and discipline I will further elaborate on in the section titled "*A Vision of What Is Right in Front of You.*")

We were blown away by what we saw. The Price Club was almost everything retail wasn't supposed to be. It was located in an old, unattractive warehouse building with very limited parking and no other retail stores

A *Vision* is much more than a statement on a piece of paper that is posted on the bulletin board in the lunchroom or highlighted in the annual report. It is, in essence, your reason for being.

• A vision must be the passion of the leader. A leader must be driven by his or her strong desire to make it become a reality.

• A vision must ultimately impact all the decisions a leader makes.

• A vision must be something that is difficult and challenging—but also attainable.

• A vision must be exciting—if you want your people to be motivated about achieving it.

The role of the leader, then, is to paint a picture of that vision in such a way that those he or she is leading will embrace it and make it their own. In that way, all of the energies of the organization are focused on the same objective. That's when the vision happens.

around it. It was dark and dingy inside; no effort had been made to make the building bright or attractive. The floors were concrete and the ceiling was exposed dark steel supports. The club carried a limited number of products, many of them food items. There was nothing special about what we saw except outstanding prices and hundreds of smiling members from one end of the building to the other, pulling large, four-wheel carts filled with merchandise. Wow! That was really exciting!

Since all Wal-Mart stores at that time were located in smaller markets, we reasoned this would be an excellent way to begin reaching and serving customers in larger metropolitan markets and start learning how to merchandise and sell food. Another very appealing aspect of the Price Club model was that we would be helping small businesses become more successful. After all, that was our own heritage and, in fact, we were still pretty small ourselves.

Sam was always for the little guy, whether it was a person, a business, or an organization. This was a way to help them. So when we got back to our offices in Bentonville, we decided to experiment with the idea of a wholesale club.

In 1983, we opened our first Sam's Club in Oklahoma City, in a building that had previously been an auto dealership. It was an instant success. The small-business owners flocked to Sam's Club, as it provided them with a new, convenient, and competitive source of inventory and supplies at really great prices. It gave Wal-Mart an entry into larger markets and a new area of retail expertise: food.

But the Sam's Club vision remained the same: improve the well-being of customers (members) through the best possible service, products, and prices.

More than twenty years later, Sam's Club is a familiar fixture in the American retail landscape—to the point that its emergence as a key component of the Wal-Mart business plan can easily be taken for granted. Perhaps the key question that Sam's Club raises is: how many companies launch major new initiatives in the midst of record-setting growth? In the previous decade, Wal-Mart had grown from $44 million to more than $2 billion in revenue—more than 1,000 percent growth. Many individuals, organizations, and companies make bold changes only when faced with setbacks and challenges, not when business is good.

Why experiment when everything is working? If it ain't broke, why fix it? While many talk about staying true to a vision, I firmly believe that Sam possessed—and instilled in his entire team—the discipline of vision: honestly evaluating yourself and your work today in light of what you want to be tomorrow.

So from a single store, to a regional chain of discount stores in small-town America, to a launch of wholesale clubs in metropolitan markets, the Wal-Mart vision continued to grow. And never content with the status quo, Sam continued to push us to better meet the needs of customers.

The Vision Grows—Supercenters Are Born

Our success with selling food in Sam's was a good indicator that we could do it in other settings. If it worked so well in Sam's, why not try food in Wal-Mart stores? We could make it even more convenient for our customers by creating a one-stop shopping experience. No need to drive around town for all your household needs—do it all in Wal-Mart, with everyday low prices on your food as well as your general merchandise.

David Glass and I hit the road again, this time up to Grand Rapids, Michigan, to visit a wonderful "combination store"—commonplace today, but revolutionary in the early eighties—founded and run by Fred Mejeirs.

Sam knew how to see the big picture—how to think big. But he also knew how to bag groceries, reload receipt paper, and greet customers—do whatever it took to take his vision as far as it could go. When was the last time you rolled up your sleeves and engaged in the frontline activities of your company?

He was a great merchant, particularly in food, a category in which he had a strong background. Mejeirs had been successfully operating combination stores in Michigan for some time. It was obvious that his stores were doing a great deal of business. We were also impressed with the many service shops they had at the front of the stores to serve a wide array of their customers' needs—from banking to family photos to hairstyling. It was on that trip that we decided that we could do the same thing in Wal-Mart.

We had a lot to learn about food and how to operate such a large store profitably. Our first experiment consisted of erecting two enormous buildings—similar in concept to a European-style "hypermarket"—in Dallas, Texas, and Kansas City, Missouri. Frankly, we overbuilt our Hypermarts and spent too much on them. We were able to generate more sales than we ever had in a Wal-Mart store, but we struggled to produce a profit because we had too much overhead.

We debated whether we could fine-tune the Hypermart model and make it successful; we finally decided to trim it back and build our first Supercenter in Washington, Missouri. It was far from perfect and needed a lot of work, but it was a great beginning. We built the Supercenters with both food and general merchandise under the same roof and included a number of service shops up front. We loved the concept, and better yet, our customers loved it. We did have a lot of growing pains, however, and had to develop the concept for several years before we began to expand.

We refused to move ahead until we were confident that the Supercenter was right for our customers. Each new version of the store was better than the last, and by the end of 1991 we began to aggressively insert Supercenters into our overall growth plans. Once again, we learned from our competition, experimented, and greatly expanded our opportunity.

The Vision Grows—The International Division Is Born

If our model worked so well in America, why not try it in another country? In 1991, we developed a relationship with Cifra, the most outstanding retailer in Mexico. Again, we had a lot to learn and suffered setbacks and disappointments along the way. For example, the leaders in Cifra did not believe that everyday low prices would work in Mexico. They were convinced that their customers were too accustomed to special pricing that showed up in the regular circulars. They did not want to depart from their high/low pricing strategy. They found it difficult to accept that a marketing strategy that worked in the U.S. would work equally as well with the customers in Mexico. In their minds, it would be costly to change the overall pricing strategy with too much risk involved. Several years later, when the leadership embraced this change, it had a dramatic impact on sales. To this day they continue to see growing sales.

But more importantly, we persevered. I believe we persevered because we were still captivated by a vision: improving the standard of living for everyday people through great products at the lowest prices. We learned the unique preferences of our customers in other countries and worked hard to serve those customers by blending the Wal-Mart culture with the culture of each separate country. While we may do many things differently country by country, we will not sacrifice our beliefs or values. Customers and associates all across the world want to be treated with respect and dignity, to be a part of something that is bigger than themselves.

In the succeeding years we became a global company by venturing into other countries. Today the International Division has continued to grow with excellent results. We have developed an amazing team of leaders from all over the world who have truly embraced the Wal-Mart Way and who are contributing significantly to the sales and profitability of the company. They are continually sharing the best practices and merchandising ideas between countries, which in turn makes each one better. For example, the chain in Great Britain taught us to effectively display more food products, and we have worked with them to develop a brand name for clothes that they have used for years in Great Britain—George. Since its introduction into the U.S. market, sales have been excellent.

In addition, a global-sourcing team has been established to look for merchandise from all over the world and share that merchandise with all countries. With Wal-Mart's global buying power, we are now able to provide merchandise for customers in all of Wal-Mart's stores and clubs the world over at low prices, helping to improve the standard of living in those countries—just as we endeavored to do first in small-town America and then throughout the United States.

Sam's vision of improving people's lives through low-cost, quality merchandise has now become a global one.

The Vision Grows—The Neighborhood Market Is Born

We have learned that not everyone likes to shop in a big Supercenter, whether it be the size of the store itself or the large parking lots. Our customers told us that if they wanted to buy only a few items or to stop for supper on their way home from work, it would be nice to run into a smaller store and get what they needed quickly—at Wal-Mart prices. If they had a sick child or needed a prescription filled in a hurry, it would be nice to have a store where they could drive to a window and get the prescription filled without waiting or getting out of their car.

This led to the development of the Neighborhood Market for the convenience of those customers with a need for speed. The Neighborhood Market is still in its infancy, but it certainly holds hope of being a wonderful complement to the Supercenter. There will always be a better way of doing business as customers' needs change, and the Wal-Mart Way means that we will do all we can to meet needs and do things better—even if it means significant change. We will expand the vision once again.

The Vision of What's Right in Front of You

Sometimes talk of vision doesn't seem very practical. It can be intimidating for all of us to think in terms of what we must do today to create a successful tomorrow.

But I believe that Sam worked at—and mastered—a simple discipline that many leaders miss or would rather avoid. As important as seeing beyond the horizon and translating that big picture for your people (the macro side of vision), successful leaders are also excellent at seeing the little things happening right now, right in front of everybody,

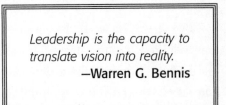

Leadership is the capacity to translate vision into reality.
—Warren G. Bennis

that others simply don't see. Sam had incredible powers of observation, and he wanted everyone on his Wal-Mart team to be the same way.

My personal tutoring on the subject from Sam came in August 1981. I hadn't been with the company very long. We were opening three stores in Huntsville, Alabama. Two of the stores had been acquired from a chain called Big K. One was on the north side and the other on the far south side of the city. Not knowing we were going to acquire that company, we had already purchased land in the center of Huntsville and had broken ground on the third Wal-Mart store there. The plan had been under way for several years, and now we were on our way to the grand opening of all three stores on the same day.

Sam and I flew out there from Bentonville very early that morning. He went to the north store and I went to the south store. He cut the ribbon on the north and I cut the ribbon on the south. We met at the store in the center of town. We greeted customers, toured the store, and met with the associates—the store looked great and we wanted to shake hands and thank our associates for doing such an excellent job.

As with most of the grand openings, there were a lot of people there, and before long Sam and I began to help bag merchandise. We handed out candy to the kids and did anything we could think of to help the customers feel more comfortable with the long lines. Sam got on the PA repeatedly, asking, "Anybody need anything?" He would then continue, "We are so sorry that you are being held up today. Next week things will settle down, and the lines won't be so long. Thank you for coming to our grand opening today and being patient with us."

We never felt we were too good to do the little things. We wanted to take care of the people and to be an example to all associates that customers come first. The chairman of the board bagging goods—what a message that sent to the people and to me as well.

Before we left town, Sam wanted to stop at a nearby competitor that was well known in the area. All it took was a first glance and I was ready to leave. Frankly, the competitor's store was terrible—rows and rows of empty shelves, boxes strewn throughout the aisles, dirty floors, merchandise out of stock, and no one to wait on us. It was an absolutely horrible-looking store. But Sam wasn't ready to leave.

He usually liked to browse and evaluate a store on his own, so he went his way and I went mine. When we finally met back at the parking lot, he said, "Don, what do you think?" (He was always asking, "What do you think?" He wanted to know our opinions—and I think he wanted us to really think!)

I said, "Sam, that was the worst store I have ever seen in my life." I told him about the rows and rows of empty shelves, boxes in the aisles, dirty floors, merchandise out of stock, and no one to wait on customers that I had seen. "They won't be tough competition at all," I continued. I still believe to this day that it's the worst store I have ever seen. But I wisely asked Sam, "What did you think?"

"Don, did you see the panty hose rack?" Sam asked.

"No, Sam, I missed it," I confessed. "I must not have gone down that aisle."

"Don, that was the best panty hose rack I have ever seen!" he exclaimed. "We don't have one that looks half as good as that one. I pulled the fixture out and it had the name of the manufacturer on the back and I wrote down their address. When we get back, I want you to call our fixture buyer and then I want you to call the manufacturer of that fixture and get them into the office. We need that rack in all our stores—it's much better than ours."

I asked, somewhat reluctantly this time, "Sam, what else did you see?"

"Don, did you see the ethnic cosmetics?"

"No, Sam, it must have been next to the panty hose rack. I missed it."

"Don, they have twelve feet of ethnic cosmetics, and we have only four feet. I wrote down some of the suppliers of the brands. When we get back, I want you to have our cosmetic buyer contact them. We need to get them in and to expand our ethnic cosmetics. They are doing a much better job then we are, Don."

That's the way Sam thought—and that's the way he taught. I will appreciate that lesson for as long as I live. It changed the whole way I look at a store. I never again looked for what was wrong with a competitor's store, but for what we could learn from it and how we could get better. That's how we strive for excellence.

Sam seldom listed all of his life and business principles; instead, he lived them. He could have written books on leadership and life. But his life was an open book and I learned by observing him that his principles were about satisfying the customer, taking care of the associates, and getting better all of the time.

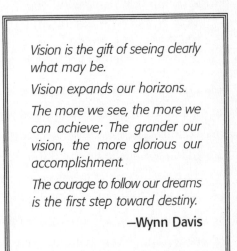

Vision is the gift of seeing clearly what may be.

Vision expands our horizons.

The more we see, the more we can achieve; The grander our vision, the more glorious our accomplishment.

The courage to follow our dreams is the first step toward destiny.

—Wynn Davis

He accomplished this through keeping his eyes and ears open to the little things that were right in front of him. And that's something all of us can do; I know I learned how on the day that I missed the panty hose rack.

As Jonathan Swift said, "Vision is seeing what others don't see."

The role of the leader, then, is to paint a picture of that vision in such a way that those he or she is leading will embrace it and make it their own. In that way, all of the energies of the organization are focused on the same objective. That's when the vision happens.

A $2 Billion Dream

A CEO of a retail chain in the East told me a personal story that illustrates Sam's thought process as related to having high expectations. It happened in a meeting the two attended together back in 1971.

There was a group of eight small regional discount store chains whose executives met several times a year to share ideas on how to improve their operations. None of their stores were in competition with each other, as they were in different geographical locations. The K-Mart chain was rapidly converting its Kresge dime stores to large discount stores, and these stores had become very tough competition for all of the small chains. The executives needed to be as sharp as they could if they wanted to continue to be successful.

> Dream lofty dreams, and as you dream, so you shall become.
> Your vision is the promise of what you shall one day be; your ideal is the prophecy of what you shall at last unveil.
> —James Lane Allen

The CEOs, the chief merchandise officers, and the chief operations officers would all meet near one of the members' best stores. They would visit the store, analyze it, and then share their observations with the company's leadership team. These critiques were very direct and to the point for the purpose of helping that chain improve its operations and service to its customers. Eventually every one of the chains would benefit from such a review by its peers.

At the end of one of these meetings in 1971, one of the CEOs thought it would be interesting to hear what each thought his company sales would be in ten years. The first CEO said that his sales were at $40 million in the past year, and he believed that they could move them up to $80 million in a decade. The next one said that his company's sales were $60 million, and he expected to be at $100 million in ten years. Another said that sales were already at $100 million, and he believed his stores could reach $160 million in that period. Finally, Sam said that Wal-Mart sales were at $44 million, and he expected that in ten years they would reach $2 billion. Everyone

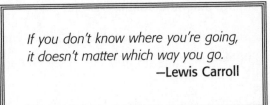

If you don't know where you're going, it doesn't matter which way you go.
—Lewis Carroll

laughed. What they didn't understand at the time was that Sam was serious. Ten years later, Wal-Mart sales exceeded $2 billion. Sam modeled the power of high expectations.

Just to show how audacious his vision was on that day in 1971, the following chart shows the sales of some of the well-known retailers in that same year:

Sears	$9.3 Billion
JC Penney	$4.2 Billion
Montgomery Ward	$2.8 Billion
K-Mart	$2.6 Billion
Woolworth	$2.5 Billion

Wal-Mart, then only the thirty-sixth-largest discount chain in the country, passed all of those other retailers one by one, eventually becoming the largest company in the world. It could happen only in America.

For reflection and action:

1. How do you go about creating a vision? Unless you are awakened in the middle of the night by a dream that presents to you a magnificent vision of your future, there's probably no better place to begin than with questions.

2. So where are you going? Based on your activities and efforts today, where are you taking your department, your organization, your industry? What is it that you really want to become? How do you want to look

ten years from now? What is the picture of the future that inspires you—and the people around you? Do you ever stop and notice the little things that others simply ignore?

3. But don't stop with questions. Capture your answers in writing with a notebook or journal and then develop a plan.

Chapter 3

The Power of Culture

Every great institution is the lengthened shadow of a single man.
His character determines the character of his organization.
—**Ralph Waldo Emerson**

Wal-Mart Way Principle #3

To build a great company, you must create a culture where everyone shares
the same values, purposes, and expectations of success.

Everyone knows what separates Wal-Mart from the competition. It's everyday low prices, right? Not so fast!

When I first arrived at Wal-Mart in 1980, that was my assessment too. But it didn't take me very long to discover a much more profound and powerful reality that Sam had set in motion. As you read this chapter, I hope that you, too, discover what I believe is the most important factor in the future success of your company or organization.

John Gardner, former secretary of health education and welfare, founder of Common Cause, a nonpartisan organization that holds elected officials accountable, and author of numerous books on leadership, has a profound understanding of the most important responsibilities leadership requires, while offering unique insights into the essence of culture:

A great civilization is a drama lived in the minds of a people. It is a shared vision, shared norms (values), shared purposes, and shared expectations! In any healthy, reasonably coherent community, people come to have shared views concerning right and wrong, better and worse. (On Leadership)

Shared vision, shared values, shared expectations, shared purposes, shared views—obviously, the key word here is "shared." In other words, Gardner believes that a successful culture is one where the people are united by common standards, and those standards provide the basis for all their actions. And that's where the role of leadership—from the boardroom to the frontline department manger—becomes so crucial. It is the leader's responsibility to "tell the story," "paint the picture," "walk the talk" of what is truly important to an organization. In great organizations, a leader's words and actions model what really matters, and as a result, everyone gets on the same page and pulls together.

One of the keys—I believe, *the* key—to Wal-Mart's success story has been our commitment to forge common ground among the hundreds of thousands of people in the organization. To a remarkable degree, associates across demographic lines of gender, age, race, creed—and even across international borders—share the same vision, the same values and beliefs, the same high expectations and purposes. Why? Because Wal-Mart works hard on nurturing a unique culture.

In an age that celebrates differences and diversity (often appropriately and for many good reasons), I am still convinced that the most successful organizations define, emphasize, and celebrate common ground. How is

> **Author Note:** *From the time I joined the team, I felt a keen sense of responsibility to preserve Wal-Mart culture, that exceptional commitment to doing what is right, especially after Sam passed away. But in truth, while leadership must set the direction, in the end, culture is everyone's responsibility. One of the most powerful dynamics for Wal-Mart is that the culture is so deeply ingrained in so many of our people that it continues to be passed on to new associates, one person and one day at a time. My prayer is that Wal-Mart associates will never quit fighting to keep the culture alive, that they will always maintain their zeal for treating people right. That is what Sam would have wanted.*

your company's culture today? Be assured, you will either create a corporate culture on purpose—or your associates will accomplish the task for you, both with and without your input!

So What Is Culture?

When we observe the different nations in the world, we readily see how differently they think and act from one another—and from our own nation. We find this reality to be both fascinating and, at times, difficult to understand—or, in a few cases, even frightening. The key to understanding any culture is discovering the dominant belief system that its people share.

In the same way, companies and organizations experience and express different cultures on the basis of their different belief systems. Some people attempt to minimize the notion of belief in general, but I would argue that all of us, whether or not we are religiously minded, hold certain foundational beliefs that affect our every relationship and decision.

Culture is the personality of an organization. Therefore, culture governs much of how people think, act, interact with others, and do their work. It is extremely powerful in determining the present and continuing success and the future direction of any organization. Culture can literally determine whether a company has a future.

A Culture of the Can-Do Attitude

Attitude is a huge component of culture, as well as the dynamic for creating and maintaining culture. You can gauge your attitude by asking, How do I view life? This is particularly illuminating when asked in the context of problems and challenges. Do you approach problems believing that you can handle them? How do you handle crisis situations? Do you see problems as roadblocks to success, or do you see them as opportunities to improve? Your answers to all of these questions will form a large part of your culture, and no one's attitude is more important to an organizational culture than that of its leaders.

The attitudes leaders have affect the way they do their jobs and the way they treat their people, and they will ultimately impact the success of their organization. Your people are watching you every day, developing perceptions of themselves, of the organization, and of you as leader, all on the basis of your attitude. By your attitude and actions, you can inspire your people to think positively and confidently as they set out to solve problems, knowing they can do it.

The Wal-Mart organizational culture begins with a positive, can-do attitude, which welcomes our customers at the front door in the person of a greeter. But it doesn't stop at being friendly at the front door. On a deeper level, we—all of our associates—truly believe we can weather the challenges and storms of the corporate world, while maintaining a reverence for small-town values—and all the while having fun! Not surprisingly, the main Wal-Mart symbol in our advertising is a happy face; we are an optimistic and hardworking people.

> I studied the lives of great men and famous women; and I found that the men and women who got to the top were those who did the jobs they had in hand, with everything they had of energy and enthusiasm and hard work.
> —Harry S. Truman

Beginning with Sam, Wal-Mart leaders have always stressed an attitude that we can get the job done, no matter how great the task. When faced with a problem or challenge, the question was always, "What are we going to do about it?" If a competitor was opening a store across the street, the response was never "Woe is us," but always "How can we improve our own store? How can we satisfy our customers better?" We viewed competition as healthy and good because it always made us better, and I believe we in turn made the competition better.

Sam's Cultural Legacy

In the early morning hours of April 5, 1992, Sam Walton passed into eternity. The founder, the entrepreneur, the leader, the legend was gone. Surely, he would be missed, and Wal-Mart would never be the same again. Many companies never recover when the founder leaves. And we certainly knew that Sam Walton could never be replaced.

At the time, many business analysts predicted that Wal-Mart would become just another company at best and that our aura of success would certainly fade during the transition to a next generation of leadership. But the Wal-Mart people had another thought in mind: "Let's show the world that not only did Sam Walton build a successful company—he built people, he built confidence, he built a belief system, and he built a culture that is enduring." And so, as a fitting tribute to him, Wal-Mart has continued to be an amazing success.

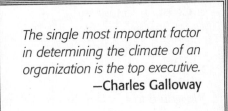

The single most important factor in determining the climate of an organization is the top executive.
—Charles Galloway

When Sam died, we had 1,945 stores in two countries, with 371,000 associates, and revenues of $43.8 billion. As of January 31, 2004, Wal-Mart had 4,906 stores in eleven countries, with 1.5 million associates, and revenues of $256.3 billion—a 600 percent rate of growth. No one would be more pleased and proud than Sam.

There is no doubt in my mind that the culture of Wal-Mart was the force that enabled us to prevail in the face of all kinds of challenges, including the loss of our leader. And we have done so, rising to become the largest company in the world. Culture is incredibly important in the success of any organization. I'm not suggesting that it is a substitute for competence; but I am emphatically saying that culture gives ongoing life to that competence and allows it to achieve all that it can.

Values Are the Beginning of Culture

The Wal-Mart culture that I have been talking about begins with our values—those things that you hold to be intrinsically good. Values identify what you stand for. In a sense, these values are the very foundation of your culture, those basic principles on which you are unwilling to compromise. All people—even thieves—have values that they live by. It is extremely important that the values in any organization be clearly articulated for and understood by everyone in that organization.

The following core values have guided Wal-Mart associates over the years and are woven into the very fabric of our culture:

- Integrity
- Respect
- Teamwork
- Communication
- Excellence
- Accountability
- Trust

We would never tolerate a breach in our integrity. From the beginning, it was wrong to lie, cheat, or steal. We did not ignore even small instances of failing to tell the truth. Leadership clearly spelled out disciplinary processes on integrity issues, including the possibility of termination.

Respect meant that all employees were to be respected no matter their positions, titles, genders, races, or religious beliefs. Your point of view was important even if you disagreed with your supervisor.

Teamwork meant that no one could do it alone. You had to depend on others, and others had to be able to depend on you.

Communication was essential at all levels in the company. This meant communication in both directions—dialogue. It meant listening as well as talking.

Excellence meant that we were always striving to improve—we had a willingness to change if it would make us better.

Accountability meant that each person was responsible for his or her personal actions. Each was expected to perform at an acceptable level.

Trust is the basis of all relationships. All associates were expected to act in a manner that would engender the trust of those they worked with: customers, suppliers, fellow associates, and members of the community.

Our values became our culture. Over time we changed everything about our company—the look of our stores and clubs, the way we transported merchandise, our merchandise assortment, our business systems, and many of our strategies—but never our values. They were the foundation of everything we did.

It is so sad today to see companies struggle and even fail because they lose sight of the vision and values that were the very reasons they were successful in the first place. When Sam passed away, we were determined not to let our values deteriorate as individuals and as a company.

What You Do Is a Reflection of What You Believe

When I first joined Wal-Mart, wherever I spoke, people wanted to know how Wal-Mart had been able to be so successful in the past, even though we were still quite a small company in comparison to the giant retailers of that day. I had observed the company both from the outside and then from the inside and developed an important list of the things we did right. My outline included our real estate strategy, our everyday low pricing of merchandise, our merchandise assortment, our people programs—and numerous other business strategies.

> *A principle is a principle. And in no case can it be watered down because of our incapacity to live it in practice. We have to strive to achieve it, and the striving should be conscious, deliberate and hard.*
>
> **—Mahatma Gandhi**

After a while, I began to realize that these strategies weren't the bottom-line driving force behind our success. First of all, I had to recognize that we certainly weren't the only company with good business practices. And over time, I had to acknowledge that strategies, to be effective, had to be fine-tuned constantly. But there was something much more fundamental that didn't change: the foundational beliefs of the company. It became very apparent to me that everything we did grew out of what we believed, and what we believed was a direct result of our values.

Values and beliefs go hand in hand and together determine how you think and act—and whether you will succeed and reach your full potential as a company. I have experienced firsthand that this is the case with Wal-Mart!

If you were to stop any associate in Wal-Mart and ask him or her what our three basic beliefs are, I am sure you would hear the following in their own words:

- We treat everyone with respect and dignity,
- We are in business to satisfy our customers, and
- We strive for excellence in all that we do.

Now, when I speak or am interviewed about the secrets of Wal-Mart's success, I begin with our beliefs. I am amazed at how many times those who aren't part of the Wal-Mart family challenge this, even minimizing the importance of our beliefs. I have had many people suggest that all this talk about beliefs sounds more like a simple bromide: Mom, apple pie, and baseball. Our beliefs are simple—no question about that—but Wal-Mart people understand what they mean and work hard at making them a reality every day.

A Culture of Respect

Treating everyone with respect and dignity means everyone. We start with our associates. We don't call them "employees"; they are associates in the true sense of the word, and there is no question in my mind that our people have made the difference in our success. We work hard to provide an environment where everyone can contribute and be successful. We treat people as more than pairs of hands to do jobs: we treat them as sources of new ideas. As Sam often said, most of the new things we do in the company come from our people.

A Culture of Customer Satisfaction

As I will address more fully in the next chapter, we treat our customers as the truly important people they are. We know that they're the real "boss." We believe that our goal is to satisfy our customers every time they are in our stores or clubs. We work hard to make every customer feel welcome, to make him or her feel like family. Our focus on the customer drives so much of what we do. As an example, our everyday low-price strategy did not grow out of a new, hot marketing trend. It developed out of our core belief that we exist to satisfy the customer. We continue to do everything in our power to add value to what the customer gets when he or she comes into a Wal-Mart store or a Sam's Club.

A Culture of Continuous Improvement

Striving for excellence means never being satisfied—always doing things to keep improving, even if it means changing everything we do. It means we never feel that we have arrived. We don't believe our press clippings. We don't get complacent and pat ourselves on the backs. We talk about what we could have done better. We believe that we can achieve extraordinary results when we strive for excellence in all we do.

Sharing the Culture

After the process of defining and developing a company's core values and beliefs, how do you keep these dynamics—the culture of an organization—alive and relevant? The obvious answer is to talk about them and do so frequently, repeating them over and over again. At Wal-Mart, we are intentional about dispersing our culture throughout the company and determined that our values and beliefs be on the mind of every associate.

Our Friday morning meetings for all officers and division heads and Saturday morning meetings for all management people serve as important times to communicate and illustrate the culture of the company to leadership. Weekly and even daily meetings in stores and warehouses provide the opportunity for all general managers to share with associates not only information about operations, but also elements of the culture. Quarterly meetings for hourly associates in the home office reiterate important aspects of our culture. Year-beginning meetings and midyear meetings for store, club, warehouse, transportation, and specialty division associates are additional opportunities for sharing our beliefs. And we have taken advantage of every single one of these opportunities to preach Wal-Mart culture.

Every company's leadership plans regular meetings to interact with its associates. The question for all companies, however, isn't whether they hold meetings. The question to ask yourself: is your culture a high enough priority to invest time in it?

Each year Wal-Mart holds its shareholders' meeting on the first Friday of June. There are usually over eighteen thousand people at the meeting, which lasts from 7:00 AM until noon. Every year, each store, club, warehouse, and home office department (including those in all international countries) sends at least one associate to these shareholders meetings as a representative of its operating unit. The associates come in on Tuesday and leave after the meeting on Friday at noon. During this time, they have meetings scheduled with the buyers and other home office associates, where they ask questions and share their ideas on how to improve the company. They have great observations and suggestions, many of which are implemented throughout the whole company. Before they go home, they are given a recap of all their suggestions and what the company is going to do about them. When they go back to their stores, they are given a chance to share with the associates in their local operations about their experiences. During this process, they not only learn more about the company and the company culture, but they actually experience it—and pass it on.

Store managers and district managers are on the front lines every day and in constant contact with our customers. It is extremely important to keep them informed on company direction, supporting and living out the company culture and excited about the company. Therefore, we believe that it is important to have personal contact with them as frequently as possible. As a result, we hold large meetings twice a year in convention centers and bring them, along with key assistant managers, in from all over the country.

Every department provides large merchandise displays, buyers give seminars on product knowledge, and other home office associates review direction in categories like marketing, operations, and personnel. General sessions include presentations by outside speakers on leadership and by senior management on company performance and the direction for the company for the upcoming months and the rest of the year. These are motivational experiences for everyone, and culture is woven into most every part of the program.

Meetings are not the only time in which we communicate our culture. Quarterly, several members of senior management, including the CEO, go into the television studio and send a televised broadcast to the stores, which is shown in our break rooms to share with all associates the state of the company. The broadcasts—spontaneous, humorous, and informal—are a fun way to let all associates in on the attitude and culture of the company.

The Saturday meeting might be the specific time in the week when Wal-Mart does its most important work as a company.

The Saturday Morning Meeting

When I first joined the company, I learned that all management in the home office gathered in a small meeting room in the back corner of the warehouse at 7:30 AM for the Saturday morning meeting.

I'll never forget my first Saturday morning meeting. After we covered sales, Sam went row by row to see if anyone had anything he or she wanted to say, and to my surprise, many of the associates did.

A manager from the construction department stood up and said that he had been at one of our stores being built in Texas. He pointed out that we were well ahead of our construction schedule in that town and that we had pulled even with a competitor who had started building a unit in the same town much earlier. He told the merchandise team that if it could ship the merchandise early to our store, we could open before our competitor did.

That blew my mind. My experience was that construction people were interested only in building a building. But there was a Wal-Mart associate who was interested in beating the competition.

The Saturday morning meeting made it possible for this construction manager to see all aspects of the business we were in and understand that we weren't building buildings—we were running stores. It also made it possible for him to educate us on his side of the business and really make a difference in our success. Needless to say, we did get the merchandise to the store early, and we did open before our competitor. How many companies are such well-oiled, tightly connected machines? That little story is a great example of how someone experienced and passed on the Wal-Mart culture to others, and how everyone was involved in the success of the stores.

As our company grew, we had to move the location of our meeting and eventually built a new auditorium. Along with our growth came other advances. Our Information-Systems Division (ISD), for example, continued to upgrade the information we received on sales and expenses for the

Probably the most well-known symbol of the Wal-Mart culture is the Wal-Mart cheer. For anyone who may not have heard the cheer, it goes like this:

Someone in front says:	The group responds:
"Give me a W"	*"W"*
"Give me an A"	*"A"*
"Give me an L"	*"L"*
"Give me a squiggly"	*"Squiggly"*
"Give me an M"	*"M"*
"Give me an A"	*"A"*
"Give me an R"	*"R"*
"Give me a T"	*"T"*
"What does that spell?"	*"WAL-MART"*
"I can't hear you!"	*"WAL-MART"*
"Whose Wal-Mart is it?"	*"It's my WAL-MART"*
"Who's number one?"	*"The customer! Always! Umph!"*

What in the world is a squiggly? First of all, it's a substitute for the hyphen. Second, it is a body action of bending the knees as if you are sitting down at the same time that you move your bent arms in a backward and forward motion. It adds some motion and fun to the cheer. This cheer is the standard beginning and ending of most every meeting in Wal-Mart. For people out-side of Wal-Mart, it seems silly to some and ridiculous to others, but they just don't understand. The cheer goes back into the 1970s and represents several very important elements of the culture. First of all, it represents teamwork; that we are in this together; that it takes each one of us. Second, it represents our informality, our enthusiasm, and the fact that we have a lot of fun. It also is a constant reminder of the fact that the customer is the reason we are in business.

past week. Sales reports listing numbers for each store and club around the world as of Friday evening at midnight were in the hands of senior leaders by 5:00 AM for their review before the meeting. ISD displayed a recap of sales by region and division on a screen in the meeting room for everyone to see. With these added elements of efficiency in place, we discussed individual store and club results on an exception basis—spending time only on the significant variances in performance—and made decisions regarding action that management may need to take.

Buyers usually had new items or categories to show to the assembled group, and sometimes the suppliers of that merchandise were invited to make comments about their products. We even had occasional fashion shows of new lines of apparel, especially at the changing of the seasons. It didn't matter whether you were in accounting, the People Division, warehousing, or real estate, everyone understood that merchandise drove sales and, as a result, everybody was immersed in merchandise during these meetings.

It was also a time to honor associates. We gave special attention to those who were celebrating anniversaries with the company anywhere from ten years on up and in five-year increments. And from time to time we brought in from the field associates who had done something special for a customer or accomplished something unusual for the company, and we as a group honored them. Some of these had participated in really spectacular events, such as saving a customer's or another associate's life.

Frequently we asked the associates if they had been in the field that week, and we asked them to share what they saw in our stores or our competitors' stores—both good and bad. We talked a lot about our competitors, with an emphasis on what they were doing better than we were and what we could learn from them.

Anyone in the audience could raise a question or share a story or an observation about something that had happened during the week that the group might find interesting. Have you ever had a dialogue with a thousand or more people? Well, we did.

This meeting usually was very positive and was an exciting pep rally for the Wal-Mart family. Sam even had some sing-alongs or talent contests when he felt we needed a little boost in morale, though we didn't hesitate to address problems and other serious matters with the whole group when appropriate. While it followed a basic pattern from week to week, the meeting's activities were very spontaneous and informal—almost anything could happen, and sometimes anything did.

It was also a time for senior leadership members to share how they felt about the business, the concerns they had, what associates should be focusing on, and what they were seeing in the stores and clubs. We also addressed principles of leadership in an informal and comfortable way. It was, again, an important time to share the company values and core beliefs. It was a time to share stories about our lessons from the past and new stories from today. It was the Wal-Mart "campfire meeting" where leadership passed on its heritage.

From time to time, we invited an outside speaker to share his or her leadership principles with us. These people's comments tended to reinforce the Wal-Mart principles and had a powerful effect coming from well-respected leaders outside our company. We invited some very well-known public figures, such as legendary stock market investor Warren Buffet, former U.S. Congressman Newt Gingrich, and General Tommy Franks, as well as the CEOs of many leading companies in the U.S. such as Herb Kelleher of Southwest Airlines and John Pepper of Procter & Gamble.

Our suppliers sometimes invited celebrities and sports figures to come and speak to the group, including such people as Mary Lou Retton, Don Shula, Hank Aaron, Nolan Ryan, Joe Montana, and Dan Marino. Musicians Marie Osmond, Amy Grant, and Steven Curtis Chapman came and entertained the associates and often shared their personal life principles with us as well. It was always exciting to have such prominent figures come and speak to us, but it was also a learning experience. Can you imagine getting all of these people to come to Bentonville, Arkansas, at 7:30 on a Saturday morning for any other reason than to speak to Wal-Mart leaders?

We're always looking for new ways to define and maintain our culture. A number of years ago—as a matter of fact, right after Sam passed away—we dedicated the first Saturday of every month to discussing and reinforcing our culture. We selected one or more of our management associates from different departments throughout the company to prepare a presentation for all home office management associates. We gave these individuals a topic several weeks in advance and asked them to share their understanding of that aspect of our culture. These sessions proved to be a constant refreshment and reminder for those associates who had been a part of the company for a long time, and they also served as a learning experience and encouragement for new associates who had recently joined Wal-Mart.

How do you keep the culture of a company alive and well? It does not happen by osmosis. You communicate, communicate, communicate—any way you can and as frequently as you can in words and in actions.

Sharing Culture in a New Market

How can a company open well over three hundred new stores and clubs every year in new markets across the country, hire four hundred to five hundred new associates in each of the stores and another two hundred associates in each of the clubs, set up and open the new units in five weeks or less, and at the same time perpetuate the culture with all those new associates?

Now add to those numbers the opening of ten to twelve new automated distribution centers averaging 1.2 million square feet, and then hiring and training five hundred to six hundred new associates for each of those centers. Be assured it takes a lot of hard work, coordination, communication—and intentionality. Here's how it is done in a Wal-Mart store or club, and similarly in one of the new distribution centers:

1. Pick the right person to be the manager.
2. Support that person with an experienced team.
3. Hire the right people.
4. Explain to each person what is expected of him or her as a part of his or her training.
5. Make the setup fun.
6. Demonstrate the culture by action from day one.
7. Work hard.

Wal-Mart doesn't hire store managers from the outside. The only associates chosen to run a new store are ones who have been with the company long enough to demonstrate that they are capable, care about people, and understand and embrace the Wal-Mart culture.

In addition to the store manager, assistant store managers from other stores are selected to become a part of the support staff for each new store. Frequently, a few experienced department managers and store associates from neighboring stores choose to move to the new store, in many cases being promoted to new positions.

The next step is to select a small group of assistant managers and department managers from other stores to come in for the first four to five weeks to be part of the training of newly hired associates for the new store. These trainers are experienced Wal-Mart associates for the most part, but the training experience sharpens them as well.

The final part of the support staff in every new store is a team called Store Planning, comprised of dedicated, hardworking, and enthusiastic specialists in new store openings. There may be only three to five members of the Store Planning team in every store, but they are pivotal in getting the store off the ground.

These associates travel from one new store to another and spend approximately six weeks in each location. Their primary responsibility is to coordinate all activities associated with opening the store. When they arrive on location, they walk into a completely empty building. They assist the store management and the visiting assistant managers in hiring all new associates, training them, setting up all fixtures, unpacking and placing all merchandise on the shelves, pricing the merchandise, putting up all signage, and seeing to a myriad of other details that give the manager a chance to hit the ground running. As important as their responsibility for details, however, from day one, they begin the process of sharing the Wal-Mart values and culture with the new associates not only verbally but, more importantly, by their actions.

Perpetuating our culture with new associates actually begins before they are even hired! Wal-Mart has been fortunate to have plenty of people who want to come work for us—many more applicants than job openings. This means that the hiring team can be selective about whom it chooses and actively look for people who will be receptive to the Wal-Mart culture. This is critical. These are the people who will be the Wal-Mart representatives to the customers. Every company wants to have people who are capable, pleasant, positive, and cooperative. We always encouraged our managers to "hire happy people." Why? The Wal-Mart culture is characterized by a positive attitude, which is easier to hire than create.

As soon as managers have assembled a crew of new associates, training begins. In addition to learning the culture, the brand-new associates will be learning to do many things they have never done before. Computers are used for some of the training and the rest is done one-on-one or in very small groups, which again reinforces the expectations and attitudes of the company. In four to five weeks, the trainers will be gone and the new team must be prepared to operate the store on its own, without the guidance of the specialized store setup team.

During the setup, everyone works hard! The Store Planning managers do many things to make the process fun and enhance the learning curve. They hold contests, dress in funny costumes, and basically do whatever it takes to get the job done and build morale. They poke fun at themselves and everyone learns the "Wal-Mart cheer" (see

> *It is a fact that you project what you are.*
> —Norman Vincent Peale

page 36). At every store opening that I have ever attended, the associates have always been fired up and ready to go. I have even been to openings where one or more members of the management team has had to shave his head or some other silly thing on a dare because the associates achieved a certain challenging goal. Part of the Wal-Mart culture is having fun, and that begins before the store is even open.

Throughout the setup process, the in-store management and the Store Planning team live the culture every single day, and they expect the new associates to observe and follow them in all they do. We put a lot of faith in our managers and planning teams and count on them to spread the culture.

Your Culture Can Help You Fail

The NASA investigating committee that reviewed the Columbia space shuttle disaster reported the following:

> *In our view, the NASA organizational culture had as much to do with this accident as the foam. Organizational culture refers to the basic values, norms, beliefs, and practices that characterize the functioning of an institution. At the most basic level, organizational culture defines the assumptions that employees make as they carry out their work. It is a powerful force that can persist through reorganizations and the change of key personnel. It can be a positive or a negative force.* (Columbia Investigation Accident Board Report. Government Published Report by NASA.)

NASA is a unique and legendary institution that still holds the distinct honor of being the only organization to put a man on the moon! So how could a culture with such a history of success have contributed to such a disaster? Apparently, over years, a simple but understandable flaw had crept into the organization. NASA workers, as a rule, did not like to give their bosses bad news, which was viewed and treated as a negative.

Your culture can sow both the seeds of success and failure in your organization.

Will the Real Leaders Please Stand Up?

We allow our management teams to have such an important role in spreading culture because we believe that the key to a strong and meaningful culture is strong leadership.

From the start, we constantly asked our leadership team to make sure our people were aware of what our culture was all about and understood what our values were. There were some individuals, however, who didn't stay with our company because they didn't agree with our values; they just didn't fit in. The best thing for them was to leave and join companies where they were in alignment with those companies' cultures. And frankly, I believe our emphasis on the Wal-Mart culture was probably a big favor to them. Why stay in a job you can't enjoy?

Let me tell you that what we believed in, we believed in very strongly. We communicated our three basic beliefs and values frequently in meetings because the culture of our company was important enough to us that we wanted to weave our values into everything we did. I see so many companies that state their values only in the associate handbook and never mention them to their people again, either in writing or verbally. How can you expect people to live out the values of a company if they are never reminded about them? Some companies do place them in hallways or on bulletin boards but never talk about them in meetings or remind their people how essential they are in successfully running their divisions, departments, or the company. Be aware that such neglect will not get the job done for your organization. A culture must be sustained by constant regeneration, and the responsibility for the culture lies with the leaders.

Sustaining the Culture

John Gardner, whom I quoted at the beginning of the chapter, says:

Three Essentials for Leadership

The key to a strong and meaningful culture is strong leadership. The task of developing and sustaining a company culture cannot be delegated—it is too important! While there are many things that leaders can do to emphasize the importance of the culture of a company, three things are essential.

1. Leaders must unequivocally believe in the culture themselves.
2. Leaders must be visible role models to all their people—in other words, leaders must "walk their talk."
3. Leaders must constantly remind people what the values really mean in the workplace, to show what these values actually look like and how they are put into practice every day on the job.

"Values always decay over time. Societies that keep their values alive do so not by escaping the process of decay, but by the powerful processes of regeneration."

When I first read this statement, I didn't like the way it sounded. In fact, I took it personally. You mean that in Wal-Mart we can't keep our focus on what made us successful in the past? Wait a second—why do values have to decay? I don't understand that. I don't agree with that.

But then it hit me. Look at our own culture in America. I think a serious decay of shared values has occurred over the past quarter of a century, a process that seems to have accelerated in the last ten to fifteen years. There no longer seems to be common ground on what is right and what is wrong. Absolutes have become blurred at best.

Why? Why would values decay over time? I think several things threaten a value system. In America, perhaps the single biggest issue is our own success. We are part of the most prosperous generation and society in history. Prosperity leads to materialism, which leads to a strong desire to get more for ourselves—selfishness. Our selfishness causes us get so wrapped up in our own needs, wants, and issues that we forget about others. Tragically, when we forget about others, we often drift away from our core values.

In the same sense, I think that in the corporate world, success can tempt us to think that we accomplished great things primarily on the basis of our own personal talent and brilliance. The value system that brought us to a point of success is no longer relevant or important. In recent years, we have seen too many corporations, which seemingly had a sound set of values in the past, somehow lose their way. Corporate prosperity has caused us to forget to renew our values. The temptation is to let prosperity erode both personal and corporate values, and this is why I agree wholeheartedly with the cliché: "The only thing more dangerous than failure is success." Too easily, we become self-satisfied, self-reliant, and arrogant.

Gardner also states, "Each generation must rediscover the living elements of its own tradition and adapt them to present realities. To assist in that process of rediscovery is one of the tasks of leadership." And many in executive offices and boardrooms have overlooked this task. We've got to help people rediscover sound values in our own organizations and in our society.

The Golden Rule

The longer I was with Wal-Mart, the more I realized how fortunate I was to be a part of a company whose standards were high—a company where leadership believed that values were to be maintained despite all circumstances, where I could blend my own values with the values that the company believed in. In fact, in all my time with Wal-Mart, no one ever even suggested that I do anything that was in conflict with my own spiritual values. I'm not saying that Wal-Mart is a Christian company, but I can unequivocally say that Sam founded the company on the Judeo-Christian principles found in the Bible. While we had a diverse workforce that included followers of the Protestant, Catholic, Jewish, Buddhist, Hindu, Islamic, and other religions, the Golden Rule was the basis of how we expected people to behave and how everyone should expect to be treated. That meant that everyone understood what was right and what was wrong in interpersonal relationships. There were absolutes. There was no confusion on those issues.

Sam understood that if you want to lead a company that exceeds the expectations of the rest of the business world and accomplish your dreams, you better set the bar high. He set high standards in his personal life and for the company—he did not abdicate his role as a leader to perpetuate good values.

I stated up front in this chapter that Wal-Mart's competitive advantage is not just merchandising and pricing strategies, but our culture. How about your company? Is your corporate culture preparing you to reach your full potential?

> So leadership, true leadership, is always about struggle. It is about two things: one, having values, and two, being willing to fight for those values. If you want to be a leader you must have values, a set of beliefs, convictions, and ideals—a vision for your country, your community, and your business. You must be willing to step into the arena and fight for those values, for that "worthy cause."
>
> —Benjamin Netanyahu,
> **Former Prime Minister of Israel**

Sam's Can-Do Hula Dance

Our year-beginning meeting in January of 1983 began as other years: with a challenge from Sam Walton. Sam challenged us to do better than we had ever done before—to raise the bar, to reach higher. He suggested to all the store managers and executives that if we treated our associates and customers better than we ever had, we would in turn experience the greatest revenue growth and highest profit margins in our corporate history. However,

> *The attitude of the individual determines the attitude of the group.*
> —John C. Maxwell

he coyly hinted, no matter how well we did, it would probably be impossible for us to reach an 8 percent pretax profit in that year. After some humorous exchanges with the audience, Sam reluctantly agreed to do a hula dance on Wall Street if we were able to reach the 8 percent mark.

Our Wal-Mart associates accepted the challenge with gusto. Everyone became engaged and worked enthusiastically to meet the goal. You know what? By the end of the year we had done it, and everyone had had a lot of fun in the process. True to his promise, on a very cold day in March of 1984, Sam shocked everyone on Wall Street by doing his hula.

This story is not a new one—it's been reported many times before. I'm not sure, however, that everyone gets the life lessons from the story. Most leaders would think that doing something like this was far below them, or that it was just a silly publicity stunt. What I learned anew is how much people can accomplish if you make work fun and get everyone involved. Sam's approachability and can-do attitude infected his whole organization. Hey, if all it took was a hula, it was a small price to pay.

For reflection and action:

1. Have you ever sat down to write out your core values and beliefs? Have you determined those issues on which you are unwilling to compromise? This need not be an extensive list. Better to be diligent with

just a few essential beliefs than to consider many things important but never really adhere to any of them.

2. Have you embraced the values of your organization? (Do you even know what they are?) Have you accepted the leadership task of being a role model in your company in word and deed? How can you improve in this area?

3. Describe in two or three sentences your company's culture. Do you practice it on purpose? Does it have you poised for success? What can you do to build a more positive corporate culture?

Chapter 4

People Make the Difference

The highest compliment leaders can receive is the one that is given by the people who work for them. It is only as we develop others that we permanently succeed.

—Harvey S. Firestone

Wal-Mart Way Principle #4

True success is achieved in direct proportion to the degree that an organization treats its people with respect and dignity—and believes in them enough to help them grow.

The Wal-Mart Way is not about stores, clubs, distribution centers, trucks, or computers. These tangible assets are all crucial ingredients in the company's business plan, but the real story of success is about people. It's about Sam Walton and other leaders who have served through the years. It's about middle managers and every single hourly associate who serves the company and customer so faithfully.

Systems, strategies, and infrastructure are all extremely important. But people make things happen! As much as any other company that I am aware of, large or small, Wal-Mart has most closely resembled a true family. Yes, we are diverse, with many different people—and different kinds of people—in many different locations doing many different things, but we have always worked together to make the company successful and be true to the vision that we share. I am not suggesting that we did everything right, but we moved quickly to correct our mistakes.

Energizing a Team

DISCARD

I know of no other company that has appreciated and respected the value of every individual the way Wal-Mart has. Now, I do know of many companies that treat their associates quite well—and I don't know of too many companies, though amazingly there are more than a few, which have built

> *Never minimize the positive impact of a pat on the back or a kind word at the right time.*

into their culture a pattern of neglect and indifference. But the issue of treating everyone in an organization with esteem is so important for success and satisfaction in the work-place, I would say that if your company evidences a greater appreciation and respect for associates than Wal-Mart, all the better and I commend you. (And I want to know what you are doing so Wal-Mart can learn and do better!)

Treating people with dignity was a key component of Sam's business plan. On the simplest of levels, he just plain liked people. Everyone. From all walks of life—rich and poor, black and white, men and women, big city and small town—he liked them all.

But Sam also shrewdly recognized the power of having everyone believe in the same vision and work toward a common goal. He realized early on that he couldn't do it all himself and that the way to be most successful would be to energize all of the team members to do and become their very best. He also accepted the fact that people generally are a lot more capable than they're given credit for, and he embraced the task of encouraging his associates by listening to them and treating them right.

Sam had a great quote on the wall in his office that was a constant reminder to me of how to treat everyone I came in contact with:

> *If you treat an individual as he is, he will stay as he is; but if you treat him as if he were as he ought to be and could be, he will become what he ought to be and could be. (Johann Wolfgang von Goethe)*

Sam understood and believed in people.

All of the people strategies we developed over the years were founded on the belief that people are valuable and perform best when they are well cared for. As a result, to say "Our people make the difference" is not just a nice-sounding motto—it has truly taken wings as a major—*the* major—

component in the Wal-Mart success story. We are a group of ordinary people who have valued each other and worked together in a way that has produced extraordinary results.

The Power of Recognition

All people deserve to be treated with respect and dignity because, after all, God created us all in His image. People need to feel that someone cares about them; that someone is listening to their ideas. The return on the investment of a "thank you" is infinite because it costs nothing—but what matters most to people are time and attention.

Several years ago, Peter Drucker, a prolific author and incredibly insightful thinker on the

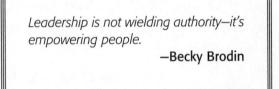

Leadership is not wielding authority—it's empowering people.

—Becky Brodin

subject of leadership, was asked what he thought were the three most important things he had learned about leadership over the years. His response was:

1. Keep it simple; don't overcomplicate anything you do.
2. The two most important phrases are "please" and "thank you."
3. Never ask who is right, but always ask what is right.

I wish every supervisor, every manager, every officer, every CEO, every leader in any organization could understand those three simple points. They don't sound that sophisticated or significant, but if they were understood and practiced, they would have a profound impact on any organization. What could be more important than motivating your people through attention and respect? How do you think those you work with would feel if they truly knew you felt they were important?

One Saturday morning in a local Wal-Mart store, I stood behind a department manager who was talking to her husband, son, and daughter. She said to them, "See this counter that Mommy set up? The store manager came by and said I did a great job."

She was already proud of the job she had done, but the fact that her store manager felt that she had done a good job and took the time to tell her was powerful. I believe those simple words of recognition and appreciation had a very positive and significant impact on her feelings toward the manager, the company, the customers—and herself! People internalize recognition and encouragement from others, and these become a self-renewing source of motivation to continue growing and achieving—and buying into a company's vision and doing a good job every day.

Recognizing someone's efforts may not seem like a big deal in the overall scheme of corporate strategies, but it was a big deal to that department manager and her family. As Ken Blanchard once said, "Who needs encouragement? Anybody who is breathing!" I totally agree with that on a personal and a professional level.

Everybody Wants to Be Somebody

Author A. L. Williams, an insurance executive with keen insight into human nature, wrote the classic book *Pushing People Up*, which I have kept on my desk as a reminder of a number of important people principles. The first chapter is titled "Everybody Wants to Be Somebody." The chapter title alone was worth the price of the book—it stopped me in my tracks and made me think differently about the world around me: everybody really does want to be recognized as an individual who can contribute something worthwhile. No matter what your job is or whom you work for, it is very important to feel important. If you feel that management genuinely cares about you and recognizes your worth, then you will be much more dedicated to that company.

Lest you think this is a simple pop-psychology technique to use to get others to do what you want, think about what it means for you to recognize fellow workers. It means:

1. You are paying attention to your environment—a common characteristic and discipline of ambitious, growing individuals.

2. You are self-assured of your own contributions and aren't caught up in petty competitions and proving you're smarter than everyone else.

3. You stand out because you are optimistic and positive—not everyone chooses to find the positives in individuals or situations.

4. You have the confidence to express yourself—and communication is the lifeblood of all good relationships and organizations.

Bottom line, recognizing others is both a matter of the heart and a discipline. I can still remember countless times when, at the end of a long and exhausting day, Sam was sitting across the break room table from an hourly associate, sipping a soft drink with him or her and discussing the morale of the store—or just as likely, something happening in that person's family or personal life. The CEO of a multibillion-dollar company doesn't have to do that. Sam wanted to. He was sincerely interested in people.

And Sam instilled that same regard for others throughout the entire Wal-Mart organization.

If You Want to Go Far . . . Go Together

When people feel good about themselves, then they can feel good about others. When people feel good about each other, they can work together as a team, and when people work as a team, they are able to accomplish exceedingly more than anyone could hope to expect. As the old African proverb reminds us: "If you want to go fast, go alone. If you want to go far, go together."

> Use power to help people. For we are given power not to advance our own purposes, nor to make a great show in the world, nor a name. There is but one just use of power, and it is to serve people.
>
> —George H. W. Bush

A key part of the Wal-Mart success story is the way our associates "go together," the way they work together and support one another. This camaraderie takes place in the stores, the clubs, the distribution centers, and the home office. All of our associates—from the department manager at a local Wal-Mart, to the order stockers, to our truck drivers, to our senior leadership members—all are vital parts of the Wal-Mart team.

I'm not saying that we're perfect; we're not. We are human beings just like people in other companies, but there is something very special about Wal-Mart associates the world over. The biggest part of that special something begins with the way management treats people. Hundreds and hundreds of times I have had associates say to me that they have never experienced the relationship they have with Wal-Mart management anywhere they previously worked.

> *I will have no man work for me who has not the capacity to become a partner.*
> —J. C. Penney

Management is accessible to them, talks to them, listens to them, and even works beside them. Wal-Mart associates are proud to be a part of the "family" and are loyal to the company.

Whether your organization is a large corporate entity or a small business with only a few employees, a winning team is born the day leaders purpose to make people feel that they are significant and that their work has value by treating them with dignity and respect.

What Do Respect and Dignity Look Like?

One of my most important lessons about treating people with respect and dignity happened in Bartlett, Tennessee, in 1990. I walked into the Wal-Mart store, and it looked great. I can walk into any Wal-Mart store and in five minutes—ten at the outside—tell you how well that store is run by what I see, what I hear, and what I observe on the part of the Wal-Mart associates. This store looked terrific: the shelves were well stocked, the store was neat and clean, and everybody was friendly and smiling. I didn't introduce myself to management; I just walked around, talking to associates and customers.

In the Infants Department, I saw three managers working together. I walked over, introduced myself, and asked what they were all doing in the same department. They pointed to the Infants' manager and said, "Oh, she just needs a little help—she is a brand-new manager and we are back here helping her for a while."

I asked who had told them to help her. They replied that no one had specifically told them to help her, but they knew she was still trying to learn the department and it was very busy that morning. "We just knew she had a lot of work to do, so we came back to help her."

What a delight to work in an environment where people don't have to be told everything that has to be done. Those associates in that store were obviously well trained and had a great attitude. They operated as a team.

I went into the lunchroom in the back of the store and asked a group of hourly associates to join me for a visit. I loved to do that every time I went into a store because it gave me an opportunity to listen to our associates and hear what was on their minds. I could easily get a feeling about how things were going in the store, how they felt the manager was

> *No man will make a great leader who wants to do it all himself, or to get all the credit for doing it.*
> **—Andrew Carnegie**

doing, and how he or she was treating them. I asked them to evaluate their store on such things as customer service, housekeeping, having products in stock, signage, morale, and other issues. I found most associates to be incredibly honest and forthright in describing their work world to me. (I think their candor is powerful testimony to the fact that Wal-Mart truly has an open communication style where most associates aren't intimidated that a "big shot" from corporate is visiting. Believe me, they aren't intimidated!) They knew they had the freedom to express themselves—and make a difference.

Sam set some dynamics in motion that were a joy to experience. Whenever I left a store, I had gained so much knowledge and encouragement from the associates, it was my humble privilege to thank them for what they were doing and encourage them. Oftentimes, I wasn't sure who had encouraged whom the most!

As we sat there that day in Bartlett, Tennessee, I told a group of hourly department managers about my experience in the Infants section and other things I had seen in their store. I told them how proud I was of how they were operating their store. One of the department managers asked me if I had seen their rest rooms.

"No—why?" I asked back. "Should I have seen your rest rooms?"

She said that they had the cleanest rest rooms in any Wal-Mart in the country. I asked her why and she told me that it was because of Gracie, the cleaning lady. She said that she took the job seriously and did fantastic work. I asked someone to go out to the sales floor and have her join us.

After a few minutes, a lady walked into the room, and immediately all of the other associates and department managers stood and gave her a standing ovation. She could barely look up because she was so embarrassed. But her shy smile showed that she was pleased. What a wonderful way of doing business—treating people with respect and dignity and honoring their hard work. The associates working in Bartlett that day taught me a wonderful lesson about respecting all of the associates, no matter what their titles or jobs might be.

Everyone Equally Important

In Wal-Mart, we say that no one is more important than anyone else. The Bartlett store showed me what that means. It means that we all have different roles and titles, but everyone in this company is just as important as everyone else. Furthermore, the best way to get people to perform is by treating them right, by making them feel important. Giving people a sense of significance is the best motivation, the best way to get people fired up about their jobs, their company, and the contributions they can make. Find little ways of impacting your people's self-esteem, and get out of their way. Then watch as they get the job done and do so with an attitude of pride to be a part of the team.

Again, this is no mere management "trick." And it's not as easy as it looks—or wouldn't everyone who wanted to be successful do it? The sad reality is that the majority of people in the work world do not feel appreciated.

Five Questions That Must Be Answered—Before They Are Asked

Since we at Wal-Mart believed from the beginning that we didn't have all the answers, we were always seeking to learn from others. From time to time, we asked a successful executive from a different industry to bring his or her senior management team to Bentonville and meet with our executive committee so that we could discuss a variety of leadership issues and learn from each other. Just think what you could learn in a discussion with such leaders as Lou Gerstner of IBM, Jack Welch of General Electric, John Pepper of Procter & Gamble, Carlie Fiorina of Hewlett Packard, or Steve Balmer

> *It is wonderful when the people believe in their leader; but it is more wonderful when the leader believes in the people!*
> —John C. Maxwell

of Microsoft, to name just a few of the executives we had in. King Solomon had it right when he said: "As iron sharpens iron, so one man sharpens another" (Prov. 27:17).

On one occasion, we met with Fred Smith, founder and CEO of Federal Express. I'll never forget one thing he shared with us. He commented that every person, at one time or another in his or her career, will have five questions that he asks himself or herself. He said that at Federal Express they feel it is important to answer those questions for everyone before the questions are even asked. His list was:

1. What is expected of me?
2. How am I doing?
3. How can I get ahead?
4. Where do I get justice?
5. Is what I am doing important?

What is expected of me? In other words, what am I supposed to be doing? What is my job? On what basis will you measure me?

How am I doing? This does not refer to my year-end evaluation, but rather how am I doing with what you asked me to do yesterday or last week or on that project I turned in to you several weeks ago. Am I doing what you asked me to do? Are the results what you wanted? Is it good? Letting your associates know how they are doing is giving ongoing, continual feedback. People want to know where they stand, if you are pleased with their performance. No associates want to be surprised when their year-end evaluations do come around. If they are surprised, then the leader has not done his or her job throughout the year. And sadly, those individuals have not had a chance to improve their performance during the year, and everyone suffers—including the company.

How can I get ahead? How can I be promoted? How can I take on more responsibility? How can I grow? How can I be challenged further? It is true that some people don't want more responsibility. They don't want another job—they are happy just where they are—but they still want to get ahead. We have some people who are cashiers, for example, and that is all they want to be, but they still want to know how they can become a senior cashier, or how they can do their job better, or how can they make more money—all legitimate ways of getting ahead. They don't want to run the company or the store or the department, but they do want to know how they can make progress, even if only for their own satisfaction.

Where can I get justice? Where do I go when things are going badly, when I think I am being treated poorly, when I think something has been done unfairly? This is an incredibly important question—and one that most companies do not even address. I think it is so important that I address it in detail in a section to come entitled "The Door Is Always Open."

Is what I am doing important? All associates want to know that they are important and that they are doing something significant. They want to know that they are contributing to something bigger than themselves. They want to know that they have more than a job, that they have a place on a winning team, and that their efforts are meaningful. One way that happens at Wal-Mart is with the amount of attention given to the customer-as-boss concept. Every associate knows how significant Wal-Mart feels it is to enhance the lifestyle of everyday people through low prices—and great customer service.

All workers ask those five questions, and the answers are vital to how they function on the job. You and I have asked all five of those questions, too, sometimes several at the same time. They form the basic framework for the dignity of a worker, and it seems to me that if you can preanswer these questions for your people on a continuing basis, you can then motivate them to perform in an above-average way.

Little Things Mean a Lot

One of our goals in the early days at Wal-Mart was to unleash the potential in all of our associates. We recognized that we didn't have all of the good ideas in the home office, so the challenge was to find a way to get associates on the front lines involved in company improvements. It wasn't one or two big things but rather many, many little things all combined together to demonstrate our intentions.

As previously mentioned, we called everyone "associates." This idea was born during Sam's brief stint with J. C. Penney prior to his military service. Back then, Penney was the only company known to call its people "associates." Many other companies have adopted that term, and now it doesn't sound quite as special. The key, of course, is not what you call your people but how you treat them. And calling our associates by that name was a constant reminder of how we were to treat them.

One day Sam came back from a trip to San Antonio, where he had seen the ID badges on the employees of a supermarket chain called Randall's that showed only their first names. He thought it was a great idea. In the next few months, we changed all our badges to show only first names, a much more personal way to refer to all of our people, whether they were management or hourly associates. That was when Sam asked all associates to begin calling him by his first name.

> There is nothing magical about it—if your employees are enjoying their jobs, if they are passionate about their work, it shows. If employees are having fun, excited about coming to work, happy to be there, the company is going to have a tremendous competitive advantage.
> —Matt Weinstein

Some individuals, out of respect for him, simply could not bring themselves to call him just "Sam." So for some he was known as "Mr. Sam."

A number of years ago, one member of our board of directors suggested that since we placed such a high priority on the value of our people, we should rename our personnel department our "people division." It didn't take very long before that became a reality. I feel that the symbols used in a business can be a factor for change if there is genuine meaning behind them. We never again referred to our human resources department; it was always the People Division. This was a small point, but relationships are made up of many small acts, and the truth is that all of us really are in the people business.

Personal Assistance for Associates

We care about our associates and want them to know that. And we recognize that our associates, like all people, have personal problems from time

Sam Walton on Wal-Mart Associates

1. If you want a successful business, your people must feel that you are working for them—not that they are working for you.
2. Share profits with all your associates, and treat them as partners. In turn, they will treat you as a partner.
3. I've always enjoyed challenging our people. If you expect great things from folks, they'll expect it from themselves. Our people have never let us down.
4. Isn't it great to see people do more than they ever dreamed they could do . . . or you thought they could do? That's the fun of this business as far as I'm concerned.
5. To push responsibility down in your organization, and to force good ideas to bubble up within it, you must listen to what our associates are trying to tell you.
6. What we need in our stores is ingenuity, morality, and honesty.
7. We get our best results from ordinary people doing an extraordinary job.
8. There is absolutely no limit to what plain, ordinary working people can accomplish—if they're given the opportunity, encouragement, and incentive to do their best.

to time. We saw how personal crises impacted their attitudes, their relationships with colleagues and customers, and their performances on the job. Sam believed that healthy families were a key to an associate's performance.

So we were open and optimistic when first introduced to a very unique organization called Resources for Living, a team of psychologists at Abilene Christian University in Abilene, Texas. Through Resources for Living, a person could get free professional counseling by calling a toll-free number. We decided to try the program out, and based on confidential feedback from our associates, we learned it was appreciated and helpful. All aspects of the program were totally confidential, and any associate or spouse of an associate could bring up any personal problems he or she was having and get expert counsel. Wal-Mart bore the entire cost of providing these counselors.

Management received a breakdown at the end of the month showing a statistical total of the types of problems the counselors dealt with: family, marriage, children, drugs, alcohol, and yes, even work. Marriages were saved, addictions were broken, families were restored, and people were even saved from suicide.

This team of counselors was also called out to stores, clubs, and distribution centers to counsel personally with associates impacted by major traumas, such as deaths in their operating units. The counselors held group meetings to assist associates in dealing with grief and sorrow and were also available to visit with any individuals who requested personal counseling.

The Door Is Always Open

Part of giving our workers dignity was giving them a voice to discuss anything that needed management attention. We strongly supported what we officially dubbed the Open Door Policy. The policy established a means for all of our associates to voice their suggestions on how we could improve our program, to express their opinions if they disagreed with something that was being done, or to address the way someone was treating them.

If associates feel they are being treated unfairly, they go directly to their immediate supervisors and try to work it out there first. If the immediate supervisors can't solve the problem—or are perceived to be the problem—

and the associates are unable to get satisfaction, then they can go directly to the manager at the next level—all the way up to the CEO if necessary. The only condition on the Open Door is that it doesn't open until the associate has first spoken to his or her immediate supervisor.

This is a remarkable program that gives confidence to our associates. It has been a key to making our company better because of the honest feedback it gives to all levels of Wal-Mart staff.

From day one, Sam let his management team know that he wanted them to be open and nondefensive. He didn't want his executives, managers, and supervisors living under the fear that this would undercut their authority and the respect associates had for them. Sam, who was humble and down-to-earth, was able to convince us that to the contrary, this program would make better managers out of us—and actually increase respect for management. Over the years, we have resolved many problems that we never would have even been aware of if one of our associates hadn't used the Open Door. I personally spent many hours responding to phone calls and letters from associates with whom I would never have had contact if not for this corporate commitment and discipline.

Just because an associate used the Open Door didn't mean that he or she was always right. But we have always tried hard to listen very carefully to all sides of an issue. Frequently, the conflict was a matter of miscommunication or misunderstanding that could be resolved by listening and guiding. I found many times that the associates just wanted someone to listen and to know that we cared about them. Unfortunately, even in Wal-Mart not everyone chose to use the Open Door, but it was always available to anyone in the company, and management reminded associates of that frequently. The important thing was that the policy gave everyone the opportunity to be heard and treated fairly.

My first experience with the Open Door came shortly after I joined the company. One of my first responsibilities with Wal-Mart was the distribution operations, which included supervision of the truck drivers. We had one truck driver who was not performing satisfactorily. He was really a decent driver, but not dependable in his personal habits. He would take a load out but mysteriously not show up at his destination, or he would arrive to work late for his outbound trip. The trucking management team followed all the correct procedures in counseling him to improve his performance. It finally got to a place where I was told, "Don, we have to terminate this man. He is not doing his job, and we have done everything we can." I looked at all the documentation and everything looked proper to me, so we fired him.

The next day, Sam came into my office and said, "Don, I understand you fired So-and-So."

I said, "Yes, Sam, he's not been performing. He's very undependable—we can't count on him. The trucking management did a good job of coaching and counseling him, and he still doesn't respond. So I agreed with the termination. By the way, how'd you hear about it?"

"Oh, he came into my office early this morning and expressed his concern," Sam answered and then said, "Don, after talking with him for a while, I want you to hire him back."

"What do you mean, Sam? He hasn't been performing for a long time." I had a lump in my throat.

"Don, I listened to the guy, and I want you to hire him back."

"Sam, I hate to go against what our people have already done. They documented all their efforts, and I think they've gone above and beyond. They worked hard on it."

"Don, hire him back."

"Sam, why would we do that? He's not a good performer."

Sam was kind to extend the Open Door to me during this conversation, and though I didn't agree with him at the time, he explained his reasoning. "Don, I'll tell you. First of all, sometimes you have to overrule your people. If you don't overrule sometimes, the Open Door does not work, and the Open Door is going to work in this company, so hire him back. The second thing, Don: if he is as bad as you say he is—and after talking to him, I'm not convinced he is—then he is going to have an ongoing problem. If he does, then you can terminate him again, and then he'll stay gone."

I had to do something I didn't want to do. I had to go to Lee Scott, the head of the trucking department at that time (and later the CEO of Wal-Mart) to instruct him to hire the truck driver back. He asked the same questions of me that I had asked of Sam. He definitely felt the same as I did, so I went through the same routine with him that Sam had gone through with me. We swallowed our pride, and the truck driver was hired back. We braced ourselves for the repercussions. But the word spread through the entire trucking department that the Open Door worked. And in this case it did. Of course, in this incident, the door swung both ways—and the driver changed his ways.

Some would say this undermined Lee's and my authority and overall weakened management. When I was telling Lee to unfire the driver, I was one who believed that! But it dramatically reinforced an important ingredient in the communication link with associates. A truck driver could have direct access to the CEO. That's really pretty special.

What's Going on at the Grassroots Level?

Direct communication with our associates has always been a priority with Wal-Mart, and we didn't wait for them to come to us. We were always trying to find new ways to hear what was on their minds.

In the 1970s, Sam initiated what became known as Grassroots Meetings. Every department in the home office, stores, clubs, warehouses, dispatch offices—all operating units—would have a meeting of all associates once every year. The purpose of the meetings was not to talk to the associates but rather to listen to them, to hear what was on their minds about the company. We tried to have at least two levels of management present to listen to what the associates had to say and try to answer any questions. We wanted to find out: What can we do to make the company better? And what can we do to help you do your job better?

Managers took notes at all meetings and posted key responses on the bulletin boards. When a manager couldn't answer the questions locally, he or she forwarded them to the home office for responses. Many of the best ideas we implemented as a company have come from those meetings. A good example was the 401(k) program, which was the recommendation of the associates.

Our point was not to just give our associates a single opportunity to express concerns and ideas each year. The Grassroots Meetings were designed to help all of our associates realize that they should be bringing things up to their supervisors and managers throughout the year.

As we got larger and it became harder for everyone who wanted to speak to do so, we added an anonymous opinion survey that contained over one hundred questions on the full gamut of subjects affecting associates and the company. We then shared a report broken down by operating unit and overall company with all associates, and we covered key issues at the next Grassroots—both the company's strong points and weak points.

Our Grassroots Meeting system was just one of the many ways we tried to communicate to our associates that we would do our best to take better care of them if they would do their best to communicate with management.

Commitment or Compliance?

When workers are given their basic human dignity, they achieve all kinds of great things for the company. But how do you measure a worker's ability to make an impact on a company?

The Gallup organization took a poll that surveyed thousands of workers in the United States. The pollsters asked a number of questions about how the people felt about their jobs and the companies they worked for. They found interesting results relating to the extent to which workers felt engaged or disengaged with their company:

- 29 percent were determined to be engaged—connected to company; work with passion.
- 54 percent were not engaged—no energy or passion; going through motions.
- 17 percent were disengaged—actively undermined accomplishments of those engaged.

(Reported in "Getting Personal in the Workplace" by Steve Crabtree, Gallup Management Journal, electronic edition, dated June 2004, pp. 1–2.)

If this survey is anywhere near indicative of how people really feel, it's very disappointing. If this same survey was conducted with Wal-Mart associates, I can't say exactly what the numbers would look like, but I am convinced of several things. The number of associates who feel engaged in the company is a lot more than 29 percent. I also know that the number of associates who are not engaged or disengaged would be a lot less than 54 percent and 17 percent, respectively. And I'm sure that any company, no matter how good it might be, will have some associates that will simply never engage.

Just think: if the leadership of an organization could find a way to get most, if not all of its people motivated, excited, and engaged, what a positive impact that could have on the business. I believe that Wal-Mart and a number of other good companies have demonstrated that it can be done. But it won't happen just because you want it to. Like everything else that is worthwhile, you have to work at it.

How Do Employees Become Engaged?

The point of this chapter so far has been to say that the way to engage the people in your organization begins with treating them right: giving them respect and dignity, genuinely caring about them as individuals, and telling them that they are important to the success of your organization (because they are). I guarantee that by doing these things, you can improve the operation of your business many times over—you can raise the 29 percent that are engaged in an average company to 50 percent or higher and cut the not-engaged and the disengaged numbers in half.

But how does that kind of atmosphere get started? First of all, it is very important to understand that it is the responsibility of leadership to set the tone in an organization and provide the environment for success; it's not the responsibility of your people to become more engaged. You certainly can't tell people to become more engaged and expect that they will.

What we have found to be most effective at Wal-Mart is to change the attitude and approach of leadership, not initiate some big, official program. Begin by embracing the fact that your people really are important and can make a difference in your business if given the chance. If that is true, then the question is: How can we make that happen—how do we give our people the opportunity to improve our business?

I remember visiting a store in south Georgia years ago. I walked through the store and visited with all the people, as I normally did. After I had finished covering my observations with the management team about how the store might improve, an assistant manager pulled me aside and said, "Thank you for telling us how to improve our store rather then telling us all of the things we're doing wrong."

They didn't need me to come in and tell them they were out of stock in a category of merchandise—they already knew that. What they needed was encouragement and practical advice on how they could correct problems and improve their operation. When I left that store in Georgia, I felt confident they would be motivated to correct the problems—not depressed because they had been chewed out.

Profit Sharing and Other Incentives

Sam and Bud weren't content with just using words to tell associates how much they were valued—they wanted to show all of the associates how much Sam and Bud appreciated their many accomplishments. They decided that the best way would be to share the company profits with them. In 1971, the Wal-Mart profit-sharing plan came into existence. All associates who had been with the company a year or longer had a percent of their annual pay put into profit-sharing accounts for them. The percent was the same no matter what positions they held. The program remains to this day and has been marvelous for the associates.

Shortly after developing the profit-sharing program, Sam and Bud decided that it would be great if they could make it possible for all associates to own Wal-Mart stock in order to grow with the company—with no hassles, no fees, and true to Sam's vision, at a discount price. So they put in place a program for all associates to buy Wal-Mart stock through a payroll-deduction plan. They could choose to set aside any amount of money and have it invested in company stock at a discounted price and not have to pay any brokerage fees. Over the years, thousands and thousands of associates—consistently more than 50 percent of all Wal-Mart associates—have taken advantage of this plan as a way to share in the growth of the company.

Through the years, Wal-Mart leadership added numerous benefit plans, as well as cash incentive plans to make it possible for associates to receive additional income based on the performance of their stores, clubs, distribution centers, dispatch offices, and the entire company. Management added all of these programs to reward the associates for their performance and the success of the company, which fostered a greater sense of engagement and involvement.

Where Do Tomorrow's Leaders Come From?

We want all levels of Wal-Mart associates to be as engaged as possible, including and not least of all, our management team. In order to prepare management talent for a growing company, we came up with a simple plan to grow our own management team. We believed in and followed the practice of promoting from within. This does not mean that we didn't hire anyone from outside the company—we sprinkled some in to meet specific needs and also recruited from college and university campuses. But we always encouraged our hourly associates to consider the opportunity to move into management. Candidates for promotion needed to be ambitious, work hard, learn their jobs, be team players, live out the culture, and demonstrate leadership ability.

We also believed in what I will call "cross-pollination." That meant that promotional opportunities weren't limited to one's store or department but included other areas of the company, including logistics, Sam's Club, Neighborhood Markets, or the International Division. This expanded the opportunities for advancement within the company immensely and was a great motivational tool for our associates. We wanted our associates to grow and be all that they could be.

As a result of our policy of in-house promotion, over three-quarters of the men and women managing Wal-Mart stores today began as hourly associates with the company. I know of no other company that even comes close to accomplishing a feat like that.

Responsibility for Self-Development

If an organization plans to promote people from within on a continuing basis, the associates need help in developing their God-given talent. In 1983, we launched the Walton Institute for the purpose of helping all levels of management in all divisions become better leaders. The purpose of the institute was not improving job skills but rather helping our people develop leadership and interpersonal skills. In addition, instructors placed a great deal of emphasis on living out the Wal-Mart culture. Over the years, more training programs have been developed for this purpose, including a computer-based learning program so that people could be taught the technical skills right in their own stores or clubs.

An organization has a responsibility to develop its people, not just in technical skills but also in the area of leadership. There is no doubt in my mind that some individuals seem to be especially gifted with a natural talent to lead. I am a strong believer, however, that leadership skills can be learned. I purposely choose the word "learned" rather than the word "taught." By that I mean it is not in the teaching that someone can develop an understanding of a principle or concept—it is in the learning.

Much of the training we did in Wal-Mart was not focused on teaching but rather on helping people to learn. Even our skill training was called CBL—computer-based learning.

If you accept that as an approach, your focus must be on the individual taking the initiative to learn everything he or she can. A company can do only so much in preparing associates for greater responsibility. As fast as Wal-Mart has grown, there has been a continuing need to produce more and more leaders. The opportunity was always there for everyone, but it was up to the individual to be prepared. I once heard a speaker say, "It's better to be prepared and not get the opportunity than to get the opportunity and not be prepared."

Wal-Mart provided schooling, mentoring by existing leaders (i.e., store managers, district managers, regional vice presidents, and so on), Dale Carnegie Training courses in the home office, evaluations focused on helping individuals grow, and a constant reminder and encouragement of the opportunities that existed in Wal-Mart.

One example of how we mentored young leaders and helped them own their personal development was through a program Sam initiated and called the "Store Within a Store." Every month each department manager in all our stores would receive a computer report of the key numbers in his or her department—sales, markdowns, margin, inventory, and so on. The store manager—sometimes with the district manager present—would sit down and review the numbers with each individual and develop merchandise plans for the upcoming months. The idea was that department managers should look at their areas as though they were stand-alone stores. This was a great learning experience, and it allowed department managers to interact with leadership on strategic issues.

Another opportunity for development comes through reading books, which is an excellent way to learn more about leadership. I always encouraged our management team to develop their own library of good business and personal development books—and to actually read as many as they possibly could. One a week? One a month? I challenged them to set their own goals and stick to them. I also encouraged them to return to their college days and underline or highlight the points that made the biggest impression on them and to refer back to those highlighted areas often. We routinely passed out copies of excellent books to our five to six thousand leaders who attended the Wal-Mart semi-annual corporate meetings.

In my opinion, the associates that were most successful over time were those who were determined to learn all they could. I always encouraged our associates to accept the personal responsibility to become sponges and absorb all they could from watching others who were successful. Watch them, study what they do and how they do it, and ask questions such as "Why?" Learn both good skills to practice and bad practices to avoid by watching others.

One Person Can Make a Difference

Is there a better way to make people feel they are important than listening to their ideas and then implementing them? Management constantly encourages associates to share their ideas about how to improve the company, reduce unnecessary costs, and satisfy the customers more effectively. We have implemented thousands of these ideas over the years. Some have been small and have impacted only a particular store, while others have impacted systems company-wide, but all the ideas have made Wal-Mart a better place to work and shop. Wal-Mart people were working on continuous improvement before it was a management catchphrase coined by the proponents of the Total Quality. It works, because it is just good common sense.

The Impact of Leadership Attitude

I was working as the computer manager of a relatively small company. One day our IBM salesman came in and told me that a company called Ben Franklin was looking for someone to run its technology department. I decided to check it out and went through the normal interview process. Several days later, I received a call and was asked to come back in because the executive vice president of the company wanted to talk to me. I was somewhat surprised because back then computers weren't a big deal, so I didn't understand why I was talking to the executive vice president of the company when I wouldn't even be working for him.

I went through the interview and didn't feel that I did very well. The drapes in his office—already dark with its mahogany paneling—were closed, and the lights were on a dim setting. Behind the mahogany desk sat this crusty old guy. He didn't get up when I walked into the room but just sat there until I walked up to the desk.

He said, "You may be seated," so I sat down. In the next thirty minutes, he proceeded to interrogate me as I had never been interrogated before. And in that short period of time, he found out everything about me. When I went home that night, I told my wife, "Whoa, did I blow it today. I mean, there's no way they'll hire me—I'll be surprised if I even hear from them again." To my surprise, a few days later I was offered the job.

Over the next year and a half as I worked for Ben Franklin, I saw the executive vice president a few times as we passed in the hallway. He always remembered my name and said, "Hi, Don," but that was it. Unfortunately, I was unhappy with my job and my supervisor and frustrated. I would go to one of the operating departments and attempt to develop a computer system based on what that specific department told me it needed to improve or reduce costs. Then my direct manager would come around and tell the department, "That's not what you need. Let me show you what you need." After going through that a few times, I was at the point where I was irritated with nearly anything—and everything—the man I worked for did.

Then one day, a good friend of mine, who went to the same church I went to, called me and said, "Don, I understand you're in computers. We need a computer person to come down to our savings and loan and run the technology department. Would you be interested in an interview?"

"Well, Bud, you caught me at a good time," I answered. "I sure would."

I went downtown to the largest savings and loan in Chicago and interviewed with him and the personnel department. Bud was executive vice president, and I would be working for him. He offered me more money than I was making at Ben Franklin. Plus, I would become assistant vice president—now that was a big deal. And the benefits didn't stop there; I'd be working for a friend. And instead of driving one hour to work each way every day, I could ride a train downtown

> If you want your employees to put forth the discretionary effort that ensures customer loyalty, you need to focus as much on your employees as you do on your customers.
>
> —Dennis McCarthy

and read the paper and do some work. On a Monday, I accepted the job and said, "I'll give my two weeks' notice on Friday."

Well, on Tuesday, I was walking down the hallway and this crusty old executive vice president stopped me and said, "Don, I'd like to visit with you for a few minutes in my office." In the year and a half since my first interview with him, I'd never been in that office again. And since I had already decided to leave the company, it didn't really matter to me if I ever visited it again.

"Tell me, how are things going?"

"Well, you know, they're okay."

"Tell me about what you are doing these days. Do you like what you do?"

He proceeded to interrogate me again and found out that I was unhappy.

I didn't tell him I was going to leave, but I told him I was not satisfied with my job there. He looked me in the eye and said, "Don, you know what? I've been around a long time. I have observed that ordinary people can get the job done if everything is going just fine and there are no bumps in the road. But I believe that an extraordinary person can get the job done no matter what the circumstances are. Don, I think you're an extraordinary person."

Wow! I had received plenty of positive affirmation in my life, but I didn't think I was an extraordinary person. I'm just running the computer department. But he thinks I'm extraordinary. Did he know I was going to give my resignation notice on Friday and was encouraging me to stay? There's no way he could have known. I'll never know why he called me into his office on that day, but I'm sure glad he did. In light of my future career in retail, I am convinced the meeting was divine Providence in my life.

After much thought and prayer, I decided I was going to stay at Ben Franklin Stores. I reluctantly called my friend and said, "Bud, I'm sorry. I've decided to stay here." I felt bad. I'd given my word. I had told him I was going to come, and now I was taking it back. I felt even worse the next Sunday when I saw him at church. He treated me fine, but I felt a strain in the relationship from my side for quite some time.

I stayed with Ben Franklin. Nothing changed with my job or the environment. I still reported to the same person. Everything was exactly the same—except my attitude. The only difference between Tuesday and Wednesday was that on Wednesday I came to work with a completely different attitude and I felt good—someone thinks that I'm an extraordinary person.

The executive vice president didn't change my reporting relationship (supervisor) until six months later. That was okay with me, though, because my whole perspective on the situation had changed, and I was determined to prove that he was right. As I think back, this one encounter caused me to approach every situation in my career with the attitude that I could do whatever needed to be done, no matter what the circumstances. In fact, nine years later I became the president of Ben Franklin, a promotion I attribute to the confidence I gained that critical Tuesday.

Has anyone ever told you that you are an extraordinary person? If so, do you remember how it made you feel? Better yet, have you ever told anyone else that he is an extraordinary person, or have you ever made anyone feel that she is extraordinary?

You and I can have a tremendous impact on the job performances of the people around us—but more importantly, we can have an impact on their entire lives. It could happen during a five-minute conversation, with just a few words of encouragement delivered at the right time and in the right way.

The greatest joys I have had in my entire career are the times when associates have come up to me, maybe even years later, and told me that I had in some way impacted their lives: a kind word at just the right time, a pat on the back for something they had done well, a word of encouragement when their spirits were down, a listening ear when they needed to talk with someone, even something I had said in a speech or a suggestion I had offered them on how they could improve what they were doing. Some have even said that they stayed with Wal-Mart because of something I had said that encouraged them to carry on.

Life offers each of us many choices. What could be more rewarding than knowing that you have positively influenced the lives of the people you have encountered? What are you waiting for?

A Friendly Idea

An associate named Lois Richard at the Wal-Mart store in Crowley, Louisiana, had a simple idea that launched a program throughout the entire Wal-Mart chain, which has become one of the most recognized hallmarks of the company. The store in Crowley had experienced a lot of shoplifting and, as a result, it had a high inventory shrinkage rate year after year.

Lois's husband was a police officer in town. One night she and her husband were talking about the problem, and she came up with a great idea. Lois went to her manager the next day and shared a new thought with him: "Since we have such a great reputation for customer service, taking good care of our customers and being a friendly store, what would happen if we put someone up at the front of the store to greet customers as they came in?

The Wal-Mart Ownership Strategy

How can you create a sense of ownership in the minds and hearts of your people? The answer is really quite simple: give them the chance to become owners. The way we have done that at Wal-Mart is fourfold:

1. Make all associates feel like partners by treating them like partners.
2. Implement their ideas that benefit the company.
3. Share a portion of the profits with everyone.
4. Give everyone easy and enhanced opportunities to purchase Wal-Mart stock and grow with the company.

This would make all of our customers feel even more welcome. At the same time, this people-greeter would be a deterrent to shoplifting as they could watch everyone going out the front door."

Fortunately, she had a store manager who listened to her. He said, "That is a great idea, Lois. Why don't you be the first greeter? Let's give it a try, but let's have everyone in the store spend a half hour up there greeting our customers." As everybody came in the front door, an associate was there to tell each how happy we were to have them in the store. After one week, everyone in town was buzzing about this people-greeter in the front of the Wal-Mart store in Crowley, and many commented to the manager how wonderful it felt to be welcomed into the store.

A week later, the district manager walked in, and Lois greeted him at the front door. He didn't understand what this was all about, so as soon as he saw the manager he said, "What in the world is she doing up there? You can't afford that labor cost. It's not in your budget." The manager suggested that the district manager talk to the customers and ask their opinions. The response from the customers was overwhelmingly positive. The district manager, who was a little skeptical when he first walked into the store, was so impressed that he decided to put people-greeters in all ten of the stores in his district.

Several weeks later, the regional vice president stopped in one of the stores and received the same treatment. He raised the same question—is having a greeter worth the labor cost?—and was amazed by the resounding answer from customers as well. Ultimately, the regional vice president put a people greeter in each of the one hundred stores in his region.

When Sam heard about it, he decided to go to Crowley to see it for himself. He loved the idea, and we placed full-time greeters throughout the entire chain. Not only did this significantly add to the friendliness of our stores, but it also helped to reduce shrinkage rates in our stores.

One lady's commitment to the Wal-Mart culture—and the listening ear management provided to her—led to the implementation of a successful new policy. This is a fantastic example of the impact one person can have on a company that cares about people and listens to their ideas. In fact, this idea has had an impact on an entire industry; many companies have now copied Lois's greeter program.

Little-Known Facts About Wal-Mart

Recognitions
- In 2003 and 2004, Wal-Mart was listed as #1 on *Fortune* magazine's "Most Admired Company in America" listing.

- In 2003 Wal-Mart Stores, Inc., received the prestigious "Corporate Patriotism Award" sponsored by the Employer Support of the Guard & Reserve (ESGR).

- On September 24, 2004, the National Committee for Employer Support of the Guard and Reserve (ESGR), in conjunction with the Secretary of Defense, honored Wal-Mart as a 2004 Secretary of Defense Employer Support Freedom Award recipient.

- In 2004, Wal-Mart was listed as one of the top 50 corporations (#5 on the list) by DiversityBusiness.com for providing multicultural business opportunities to diverse suppliers based on a poll of more than 200,000 diversity business owners across the U.S.

- In 2004, *Black Collegian* magazine listed Wal-Mart as one of the top diversity employers.

- *Hispanic* magazine ranked Wal-Mart Stores, Inc. among the top 100 companies providing most opportunities for Hispanics in 2004.

- *Vista* magazine announced in 2004 that Wal-Mart was named among its Top Family Friendly Companies for Hispanics.

- *Latin Trade Reader* named Wal-Mart among Latin America's 25 Most-Respected Employers in 2004.

- In 2004, Wal-Mart was named by *Asian Enterprise* magazine as one of the top ten companies for Asian Americans.

- Wal-Mart received the 2002 Ron Brown Award, the highest Presidential Award recognizing outstanding achievement in employee relations and community initiatives.

- In a poll sponsored by *Career and Disabled* magazine in 2004, Wal-Mart was recognized as one of the top companies in the nation for providing a positive working environment for people with disabilities.

- ASDA was named the best place to work in the United Kingdom by *Fortune* magazine in 2004.

- Wal-Mart Canada was named the best retailer to work for in Canada by Report on Business Magazine in 2003 and 2004.

Employment/Job Creation

- Wal-Mart employs more than 1.2 million associates in the United States and more than 385,000 associates internationally as of December 2004.

- Wal-Mart Stores, Inc. plans to create more than 100,000 new jobs in the United States during 2005.

- In Mexico, Wal-Mart de Mexico plans to create more than 11,000 new jobs in 2005.

- Each new supercenter in the U.S. creates approximately 400–500 jobs and 74 percent of Wal-Mart's hourly store associates in the United States are full-time. That's well above the 20–40 percent typically found in the retail industry.

- Each new SAM'S CLUB creates approximately 160–175 jobs.

- Typically, each new distribution center begins with 450–500 new jobs and many of them grow to over 900 jobs within a year. (Virtually all of these jobs are full-time.)

• Wal-Mart promotes from within. Seventy-six percent of Wal-Mart's store management team started in hourly positions with the company.

• Wal-Mart Stores, Inc. promoted more than 9,000 hourly associates to management during the past year and many of those jobs did not require a college degree.

• Frequently, Wal-Mart receives thousands of applications for our 400–500 job openings at a new supercenter. In New York, Wal-Mart estimated more than 15,000 applicants applied for 400 jobs at a new store.

• Wal-Mart is a leading employer of African Americans (over 206,000 African American associates) and Hispanics (over 133,600 Hispanic associates) in the U.S.

• In the United States, Wal-Mart is one of the largest employers of senior citizens.

• Wal-Mart is proud of the more than 38,300 associates who have served in the military. The company provides continuation of benefits and makes up any difference between military pay and Wal-Mart wages for associates who are called to active duty.

Wage/Benefits for Associates

• Our average wage for regular full-time hourly associates—such as cashiers, stockers and sales associates—is almost twice the federal minimum wage. No one at Wal-Mart is paid at or below the federal minimum wage.

• Wal-Mart benefits—available to full and part-time associates— include healthcare insurance with no lifetime maximum.

• Wal-Mart insures more than 900,000 Americans, who pay as little as $17.50 for individual coverage and $70.50 for family coverage bi-weekly.

• Associates enrolled in the plan also have access to world class health care at the Mayo Clinic, Stanford University Hospital, Johns Hopkins University Hospital and many other health care facilities, all without insurance approval.

- Other benefits include a profit sharing/401(k) plan, merchandise discounts, company-paid life insurance, vacation pay and pay differential for those in active military service.

- More than half of Wal-Mart's associates own company stock through our associate purchase plan.

- Wal-Mart projects that the company will spend $4.1 billion on benefits for our associates in fiscal year 2005.

- Currently, 86 percent of Wal-Mart associates surveyed have medical insurance; 56 percent of those with coverage received healthcare insurance through Wal-Mart and the remainder received healthcare insurance through another source such as another employer, a family member, the military, or Medicare.

For reflection and action:

1. How would you rate yourself in the following areas?
    - I am interested in the well-being of others.
    - I believe that others offer perspectives and talents I don't have.
    - I am a good listener.
    - I am open to new ideas—even if they are not my own.
    - I am careful to take note of how happy and satisfied others are.
    - I am an encourager.

2. Write down three or four ways you would like to grow—and help your organization grow—in people skills and attitudes.

Chapter 5

The Customer Is the Boss

It is not the employer who pays the wages. Employers only handle the money. It is the customer who pays the wages.

—*Henry Ford*

Wal-Mart Way Principle #5

You will succeed when you make a commitment to help your customers succeed first.

It doesn't matter what business you are in, it is essential that the primary motivation and driving force behind everything you do is based on the impact it will have on your customer. Whenever we discussed a major change in any operating strategy at Wal-Mart, one of the first questions raised was: "How will this affect the customer?" It didn't matter if it was in an executive committee meeting, a staff meeting, or a store meeting. Discussions always began and ended with the customer.

The customer is the only reason any of us are in business. And though none of us will ever attain perfection in providing the greatest value and service to the customer, from the beginning at Wal-Mart it was always the preeminent part of our decision-making process. It was the focus of everything we did.

To succeed, it is essential that everyone in an organization be passionate about the customer.

Customer Service—More Than Lip Service

Unfortunately, in too many companies, the leaders say all the right things, but they don't practice what they preach. They offer lip service regarding customer service, but in reality, the customer is the last one they consider; instead it's sales revenues, profits, the stock price, marketing, shareholder value, and other business considerations. Don't get me wrong: all aspects of your business plan are incredibly important for your long-term success. And all leaders must navigate the delicate balance between their customers and shareholders. But I argue that you won't reach your potential as a company or organization until you put your customers first.

There are always many voices that speak up for profitability, but companies need just as many advocates for the customer, those who will always speak up about our responsibilities to the customer. There are generally fewer of those voices—and they often get drowned out in the clamoring for valid, yet derivative business matters. How can issues like profitability be derivative? Simple. They don't happen without a loyal customer base!

Sam created a culture and environment in Wal-Mart where leadership encouraged every person at every level to serve as the voice of the customer. You can't go through a day working at Wal-Mart without someone or something constantly reminding you of whom you really work for. Sam always said that we all had the same boss: the customer. As a matter of fact, that's the only time we used the term "boss." (To this day, I don't like the word *boss* applied to a supervisor, manager, or leader. It is a word from the past, a residue of an autocratic style of leadership that does not reflect more enlightened understandings of leadership today.) The term *boss* wasn't thrown around carelessly in Wal-Mart, and referring to our customers as our "boss" meant that we took our relationship with them very, very seriously.

Wal-Mart Merchandising Strategy—The Family Store

Customers come to our stores and wholesale clubs for the merchandise we offer for sale. Since the customers are the boss, our merchandising strategy focuses on what they need, what they want to buy. Wal-Mart buyers make thousands of decisions every single day on what to buy for those customers. From the very beginning, we needed to establish ground rules for our buyers to follow as they made those decisions.

What kind of a store are we? We are a family store. We want to supply the everyday needs of every member of the family. Furthermore, we want to offer merchandise that every family in the country needs, regardless of its socioeconomic level. In other words, every single family is a candidate to be a Wal-Mart shopper for something; therefore, we carry most of the items needed to run a household, with heavy emphasis on consumable items. After all, we have one hundred million family members shop in our stores each week.

We recognized that we couldn't be everything to everybody, so we made choices to focus primarily on basics. That meant that we would stay away from the higher-priced lines, such as dress clothes and other high-end merchandise lines. In the apparel area, for example, we chose to sell basic sportswear and casual office wear. At the same time, it was extremely important for us to always offer quality to our customers, and therefore we emphasized buying name-brand merchandise wherever possible, and we never sold seconds.

Another dimension to our merchandising strategy is that we always offered as wide an assortment of merchandise as possible. Today, in an average Wal-Mart store we have more than eighty thousand individual items, and more than one hundred thousand items in a Supercenter, approximately 30 percent more than our competitors. Because of the diversity of our markets, our stores actually choose from more than four hundred thousand items. Our customers told us that's what they want-

> *Whoever renders service to many puts himself in line for greatness—great wealth, great return, great satisfaction, great reputation, and great joy.*
>
> —Jim Rohn

ed. Every market research report I have ever seen shows that customers, in general, want a large assortment.

Recognizing that many of our customers are average American families working hard to make ends meet, we believe that low prices are essential, and we never stop working to keep our prices low. Coupling our buying strategy with our pricing strategy, as a result of our overall merchandising strategy we have been able to achieve a dominant market position in categories as diverse as dog food, fabric and crafts, toys, men's and boys' underwear and socks, and music and videos.

Sam's Clubs—A Different Customer and Approach

The merchandising strategy in Sam's Clubs is completely different from that in Wal-Mart stores. Since the primary customer has joined the store, making him or her a "member," and he is usually a small-business owner, the breadth of assortment is not as important as in family-driven stores. Each club carries between thirty-five hundred and four thousand individual items. What is important is that we offer the most common items our members need in their businesses and carry them in mass quantities and in larger servings sizes. By limiting the assortment and handling the merchandise by full pallet loads, we keep costs at a minimum, thereby offering prices to the members at the lowest level possible.

As a special courtesy to business owners and in respect for their time, Sam's also sets certain hours in the morning when only business owners can shop. Since they purchase large quantities of items and usually load them on flatbed hand trucks, it makes it easier for them to get what they need without other shoppers and families crowding the aisles.

Sam's merchandise assortment is also geared to higher-priced items for individual members that are usually sold in department stores. We sell these items at unbelievably low prices, offering a huge savings over what a member would pay anywhere else. This practice attracts many members who regularly do much of their shopping in department stores and specialty shops.

Another important concept of the Sam's Club strategy is to always have new merchandise flowing in for a limited period of time and then replacing it with other new items. This creates a sense of a "treasure hunt" every time a member shops in the club because there is always something new. The expect-the-unexpected feel is a great appeal to the individual members as well as the business owners for their personal needs. Periodically, for example, a "road show" of items such as fine furniture, pool tables, or luxury gifts will be brought into a club for several weeks and then moved to another club. The novelty also adds to the excitement of shopping in a Sam's Club.

As you can see, the merchandising strategies of Wal-Mart's different divisions are not the same, but the thinking processes behind the strategies are identical. The common threads are:

- Focusing on the customers by providing the merchandise they are asking for, not what you may want to sell them.
- Driving down the costs of operations.
- Keeping prices as low as possible.
- Creating a fun and friendly shopping environment.

The Power of Accountability

Over the years, we learned that every time we drifted from these basic fundamentals of merchandising, our business suffered, and we had to get back to square one. Sometimes it's difficult to reverse direction and correct yourself, and that's where some once-great companies have floundered to the point of extinction. They were either unwilling or unable to admit that they had slipped in their relevance to the market.

Anytime our sales fell below certain defined expectations, we had to remind ourselves that it wasn't the customers or our competition that was to blame: it was us. As Julius Caesar said to Brutus in Shakespeare's play: "The fault, dear Brutus, is not in the stars, but in ourselves."

Addition of Private-Label Merchandise

Wal-Mart has always been, and most likely will remain, a retailer that supports national and international brand merchandise. In the minds of many consumers, brands are synonymous with quality. Therefore, our strategy was to offer primarily name brands at everyday low discount prices, thereby providing our customers with genuine value and with a direct comparison to our competitors. We were always proud of our prices and never shied away from comparisons.

In the early years, we offered a limited number of private-label items, but they represented only a small portion of our sales. The most familiar private-label item we carried was dog food named Ol' Roy after Sam Walton's favorite hunting dog.

In the late 1980s, however, the prices of numerous national brand items were continuing to increase beyond levels that we believed to be reasonable. Even at our comparatively lower prices, we didn't believe we were providing adequate value for our customers. Wal-Mart management determined that our customers should have the option to buy name-brand quality at a reasonable cost. As a result, the company embarked on the development of several lines of store-brand or private-label items that would be at least comparable to national brands in quality, but significantly lower in price. This was a major departure from the historical practice of private-label merchandise in retailing. The standard at that time for private-label merchandise was definitely lower price, but also significantly lower quality sold in unattractive packaging.

Each item Wal-Mart selected, whether it was food or one of the general merchandise categories, was sent out to independent testing laboratories to ensure that the quality met our specifications and our customers' expectations. Only the highest level of quality was acceptable. In fact, we aimed to exceed the quality of the name-brand items whenever possible. Packaging was also extremely important. With the package being the window to the product, we thought it critical that the package represent the same quality as the product inside. As a result of our rigorous efforts, we introduced to U.S. retailing private-label items with not only great quality and low prices, but also in extremely attractive packages with very colorful graphics.

Why do I keep emphasizing the packaging? What does that have to do with quality? What does that have to do with putting the customer first? What made this so important to Wal-Mart was that we were attempting to affirm that cost-conscious people deserve and can afford quality items, without the emotionally negative stigma associated with such inferior packaging. Remember, Sam started in the retail industry when people living in small towns did not have an equal shopping experience with those living in larger metropolitan areas.

We carefully reviewed and tested each item during development to make sure that it was exactly what our customers were looking for and represented a genuine value. We added easy-open lids and zippers if needed and chose sizes that provided the best value relationship between quantity and price to the customer. Sam's Clubs also began developing its own private-label merchandise and selling some of the Wal-Mart brands to their members.

As each of these fine brands continued to gain our customers' acceptance and trust, sales increased, and as an unexpected outcome, our private labels became name brands. The next step was to introduce these offerings to our International Division, and they have likewise become international brands in countries all over the world. This has allowed us to expand our original goal of providing U.S. customers with a low-priced, quality alternative to name brands and giving that same opportunity to international customers worldwide. Today many of the company's store brands, such as Ol' Roy and Great Value, have become the number-one brands in the U.S. and are growing in acceptance globally.

Family Store Values

As a family store, we made merchandising decisions that cost us sales because they were in conflict with our values and our heritage. We chose not to carry certain magazines that we did not find appropriate for family. We decided that we should not stock CDs that had suggestive pictures on the cover or vulgar words in the lyrics; the same rule applied for games and videos. While this caused quite a stir in the record industry and the media at

> *Wal-Mart is the greatest thing that ever happened to low income Americans. They can stretch their dollars and afford things they otherwise couldn't.*
> —W. Michael Cox, chief economist, Federal Reserve Bank of Dallas, the *New York Times*, December 2003

first, companies began producing edited versions that we would sell, and we even became involved in some of the coding and rating systems of the music and gaming industry. Eventually, other discounters chose to sell the edited versions in their stores as well.

While you can't please everyone, and I'm sure we have stocked merchandise in our stores that we weren't fully aware of content-wise, we have consistently attempted to honor the morals and sensibilities of the everyday individuals who shop in our stores and clubs. With our emphasis on being a family store, we were particularly sensitive in our merchandising decision not to embarrass parents who bring their children into our stores while shopping.

We Are All Merchants First—The VPI Contest

Sam Walton was a great merchant—he had an uncanny sense of what people wanted to buy—and he wanted everyone in the company to be a great merchant also, from our buyers to our hourly associates. We talked about merchandise all the time. In many of our meetings, we showed all of our people the new and "hot" items and categories. I strongly believe that if you want your associates to have a real interest in your company, you have to expose them to your products. A common saying in our company was "We are merchants first." That was even a motto in the technology department.

One of the most successful—and entertaining—programs we developed was called "VPI," which stands for a Volume-Producing Item. Every department manager in every store selects an item that he or she believes can become a fast seller. They then feature the items in their stores, perhaps on an end cap or with special signage, and keep track of the sales of that item. Meanwhile, the store managers and assistants also pick an item. So all throughout the store a friendly competition begins—to see whose item does the best. At the home office, all officers pick an item, and so do many of the home office departments.

Each month, at a Saturday morning meeting, management shares a recap with the entire group of the year-to-date standings of each individual. A great deal of good-natured competition and kidding goes on—who kids whom depends on who is in what place. At the end of the year, there is a big ceremony where the individual who has chosen the worst-performing item receives the FISH award. You have heard of different methods of valuing inventory—FIFO means First-In-First-Out; LIFO means Last-In-First-Out. FISH is a Wal-Mart-only method used just for the VPI contest that means First-In-Still-Here. The dubious winner of that award is presented with a large, smelly fish on a platter in front of about five thousand to six thousand associates at a year-beginning meeting.

It's a fun exercise that feels a little like a Super Bowl party with friends who are rooting for opposite teams. But the whole point of VPI is to focus everyone's attention on merchandise. Many things in any business can be a lot of fun but also contain a great lesson. VPI and the dreaded FISH award already belong to Wal-Mart. You need to create your own programs that combine entertainment and education. What we needed to accomplish was keeping the entire company in the loop concerning merchandise.

Customer Service—or Customer Satisfaction?

Despite the counsel of seminar speakers and textbook writers, customer service is not how you identify with your customers. If your company is to succeed, your emphasis must rather be on customer satisfaction. You can serve people without satisfying them, but it's impossible to satisfy them without serving them. Satisfaction is the goal, and at Wal-Mart we determined to accept nothing short of that because we knew that when customers are satisfied over a long period of time, that's when we create trust. And trust is

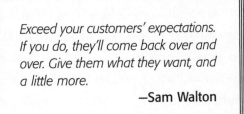

Exceed your customers' expectations. If you do, they'll come back over and over. Give them what they want, and a little more.

—Sam Walton

the foundation of every relationship in life. I can't emphasize that enough or repeat it enough times, and yet companies so easily take it for granted.

In every market research survey we ever commissioned, customers always rated Wal-Mart the company they most trusted. It is in the process of satisfying customers that you create trust, and ultimately trust leads to loyalty. In any business, customer loyalty can't be bought—it can only be earned, and trust is the most important reason customers keep coming back. You can spend a lot of time and money trying to attract new customers, and yes, every business must do that, but it is even more important—and costs a lot less money—to keep the customers you already have.

Treat Customers As If They Were Guests in Your Home

A lot more than merchandise choices and pricing goes into providing a great shopping experience for your customers. First of all, a unique shopping experience for most people includes a friendly atmosphere. Sounds too simple, but think about what goes into motivating tens of thousands of associates in thousands of locations to be friendly to every single customer every day. Many of us struggle to pull off that feat in our own homes!

An analyst asked David Glass, during his tenure as president and CEO of Wal-Mart, "How do you run a company that has sales of over $100 billion?" David's reply was, "I don't have the slightest idea; we just do it one store at a time, one customer at a time, one day at a time." While that sounds too simplistic, possibly even humorous, it's a fantastic response. The point is that you must concentrate all of your energies on satisfying every single customer on every single visit he or she makes to your store every single day.

Our People Make the Difference

A friendly atmosphere begins with wonderfully friendly associates in our stores. They are the heart and soul of Wart-Mart's customer-satisfaction program. They are the ones who meet and greet each customer each day. They are the ones who represent Wal-Mart to every customer. If they are outgoing and pleasant, then Wal-Mart is outgoing and pleasant; if they are curt and distant and distracted, then Wal-Mart is curt and distant and distracted. The associates are literally the face, the hands, and the voice of Wal-Mart. It is what the associates in the stores do that is responsible for the outstanding reputation we have enjoyed over the years. They are friendly even when dealing with angry and unfriendly customers, and even when they are dealing with their own personal problems at home or work.

I mentioned earlier that you can't work a single day without someone or something reminding you how important the customer is. Our associates have bought into Sam's vision. They believe in the company and what we stand for. And it shows up every time a customer enters the store.

How do you create a friendly workforce? One of the simplest ways is to hire cheerful people. For Wal-Mart then, our friendliness begins with the hiring process. We look for positive, outgoing people—people we would enjoy talking to and working with. So we ask our associates if they have friends that would like to work here—people they would recommend. In many of our stores, the hiring committee is made up of hourly associates who have demonstrated that they are pleasant and hardworking and care about other people. They generally make excellent choices about who would

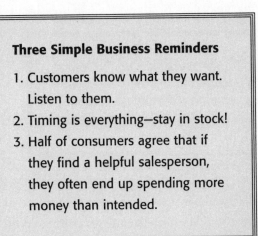

Three Simple Business Reminders

1. Customers know what they want. Listen to them.
2. Timing is everything—stay in stock!
3. Half of consumers agree that if they find a helpful salesperson, they often end up spending more money than intended.

fit in well at Wal-Mart. We tell them to hire happy people and then release them on the customers.

In the chapter "The Power of Culture," I mentioned that not everyone who has come to work for Wal-Mart buys into the Wal-Mart culture, and because of the ongoing emphasis we put on our culture, they often don't stick around. That is particularly the case with friendliness. Some people think that smiling and trying to be helpful is a bit too naïve, unsophisticated, and even sappy for their personas. That's okay. These people simply need to find a company or organization that presents a different demeanor. Wal-Mart is small-town friendly.

What's the Ten-Foot Rule?

Sam instituted what he called the Ten-Foot Rule. When you come within ten feet of a customer, no matter what you are doing, look up, look the customer in the eye, and speak to him. If you are asked where something is, instead of pointing to the aisle or trying to explain where it is, take him to the merchandise. This amazes many customers.

As a result, Wal-Mart customers feel as if they belong in our stores. Our customers are frequently in our stores several times a week—some even daily.

Our associates actually get to know the names of many of their customers, and people love to be called by name. Customers come in looking for certain associates to talk with when they are in the store. Frequently, customers refer to a particular store as "my Wal-Mart." They actually feel a sense of ownership, which leads to a real family atmosphere and very positively influences their entire shopping experience. Our advertising agency frequently interviews customers in our stores and asks them what they like about Wal-Mart and why they shop there. One customer they interviewed responded, "I trust Wal-Mart; it's like my grandma told me to shop here." The associates' friendliness makes the customers feel at home and, we believe, really sets Wal-Mart apart from our competitors.

> *Businesses planned for service are apt to succeed; businesses planned for profit are apt to fail.*
> —Nicholas Murray Butler

Little Things Mean a Lot

Customer loyalty doesn't just happen; you have to work on it every day. It isn't only big things; it's a lot of little things done over and over again. Over time, these little things demonstrate to your customers that you really care about them and are genuinely interested in satisfying them. It is important to understand that you don't do it only to increase sales; you do it because it's the right thing to do.

It means having a people-greeter in every Wal-Mart store to welcome every customer when he or she comes in the front door. It means that it is incredibly important to be in stock on every item, so we don't disappoint any customer. In fact, "in stock" may be the most important element of customer satisfaction because, obviously, customers come in to buy merchandise. If they can't find what they came for, they will leave disappointed. If that happens too frequently, they will shop somewhere else. That's why Wal-Mart puts so much emphasis on execution. You can be a pretty store—brightly lit, clean and attractive, with friendly sales clerks—but if you are out of stock, the customers will leave your store unhappy.

It means accepting merchandise back if the customer is not satisfied. If something doesn't fit, is the wrong color, or doesn't work, bring it back without a hassle—just have your sales receipt. We have tried to eliminate the hassle and make it easy. (Unfortunately, however, some customers try to take advantage of our liberal returns policy, and this has caused the company to tighten up on returns so that our honest customers are not penalized by increased prices.)

It means creating an atmosphere of excitement in every store. Our associates love doing fun things like dressing up in costumes for holidays, decorating their stores for the different seasons, displaying balloons and signs, having style shows, or having local organizations do bake sales and other fund-raisers out front. These are high energy activities that lift the spirits of the customers and associates alike and simultaneously create a festive atmosphere in the stores. They make Wal-Mart a fun place to shop. Let me ask you: Do your customers enjoy doing business with you?

Prices Aren't Everything, but They Come Close

Wal-Mart has established a great reputation for low prices. The real key is everyday low prices—not just advertised low prices on a few selected items for a week or weekend. I remember in past years going to seminars and conferences with other retailers and discussing our respective marketing strategies. They talked about their weekly or biweekly advertising circulars and how those were their bread-and-butter method for drawing customers into their stores. Then they would politely acknowledge our idea of everyday low prices as a strategy for attracting customers but never sounded too impressed.

What our competitors didn't realize was that little by little, we were drawing their customers away from them, because customers were finding that on a day-in and day-out basis, they were paying less for their purchases at Wal-Mart and were significantly reducing their cost of living. This seriously undermined classic retail strategies of the loss leader and bait and switch with customers, who were getting a better value from everyday low prices. No matter what business you are in, value is what your customers are looking for.

You can't maintain low prices without low costs, so Wal-Mart has always worked closely with suppliers to drive costs out of the system (I'll describe this more fully in chapter 10, "Creating Supplier Relations"). When we cut costs, we pass this savings on to the customer and have what we call price "rollbacks." We advertise rollbacks to draw the attention of the customer to the fact that we have reduced the price of an item or a category. This has been a tremendous reinforcement to our everyday low-price image and has further reduced the cost of living of our customers.

To completely understand this strong emphasis on setting the lowest prices possible on the items in our stores, you need to understand that we really do believe in Sam's vision of improving the lifestyle of everyday Americans—and people throughout the world. We came to view ourselves as the "agent" of the customers. As their agent, we believed that it was our

> *World-class leaders know that customer loyalty, employee commitment, and operating efficiency are all essential elements of business success. Therefore, they refuse to trade off one for another.*
>
> —George Labovitz

job to buy wisely for our customers, not just sell to them. This is a completely different approach from what is common in other organizations. Though simple, it is revolutionary, and many leaders in the retail industry still do not understand it. Our role as the customers' agent explains why we sometimes have an item that our closest competitor prices at $19.95, which we price for just $14.86. I have been asked many, many times why we don't raise the price to, say, $16 or $17.95. We would still be pricing lower than the competition but increase our margins and make more money. Surely the market would bear the extra buck or two. As hard as it is for many to understand, we actually try to sell our merchandise as low as we can, not as high as we can. Why? We are the agent for the customer. And by the way, our customers know what we are trying to do. They have come to recognize that "Everyday low prices" is more than a slogan.

The Marketing of Wal-Mart

A carefully thought-out marketing strategy is a key element in the success of any organization. Marketing is not to be confused with advertising. Advertising is only one part of marketing, albeit an important part. But marketing is the total face you show to your existing and potential customers—your product, your place of purchase, your promotion, and your pricing. What is it you really want customers and potential customers to think about when they hear your name? What image do you want to appear in their minds at the thought of you?

Marketing begins with the product itself. What does it look like? How does it operate, and who are the potential users? What makes it unique or different? How is it packaged? Why would someone want to buy it?

The next step in marketing involves getting the product to the customers—that is, your place (or point) of purchase. Are you brick-and-mortar? Internet? Both? What channels will you use to distribute your product?

And then there's promotion. How will your products and services—how will you—be advertised? Newspapers, magazines, radio, TV, the Internet, word of mouth, home parties, door-to-door?

One last element that will clearly impact sales of the product is the pricing strategy you will employ. Obviously, a key factor in that decision is the cost to produce and deliver the product. The ultimate goal of Wal-Mart is to reduce the cost on a continuing basis in order to provide value to the customer and a fair return to the company.

Finally, taking the previous four components of marketing into account, the overall company message must be clear and easily understood. It must succinctly convey the message you want your audience to hear. It must be believable and truthful, as well as compelling, without overstating your case. Don't promise something you can't deliver.

Marketing must be unique and different, dramatic, or even humorous in order to attract attention. If the marketing program is carefully and deliberately crafted, it can give any organization a powerful competitive advantage and add significantly to sales.

Unique and Compelling Wal-Mart Themes

The Wal-Mart marketing strategy has been unique among retailers. The product, as I have explained, is a store designed to satisfy customers by offering the everyday household needs of families in a friendly and fun atmosphere; it is a wide assortment of merchandise, with an emphasis on brand-name products; it is friendliness of the associates; and it is everyday low pricing. (Always.)

In the early years, Wal-Mart advertised, as did most of the retail industry, primarily in local newspapers and in monthly circulars. Many of the items selected were shown at reduced prices. Over time, it became apparent that reducing prices on several hundred selected items wasn't completely consistent with—or nearly as effective as—everyday low prices, so we decided to change that element of our advertising. Television became the primary medium for sharing who we were, and we changed the monthly circular to feature items at their everyday low prices, thereby reinforcing our pricing strategy. We designed the television spots to show Wal-Mart as a friendly place to shop, where you could find the merchandise you needed every day for your home and family; as a place where you could depend on prices being low every day and even being consistently rolled back; as a place where you could bump into your neighbors and leave satisfied with the quality and price of your purchases.

Another strategic element in Wal-Mart promotion and advertising plans was that we kept costs down and passed the savings on to the customers. We consistently spent at least 2 percent less than our major competitors in our marketing budget. In the retailing business, this is a tremendous cost advantage to have over your competition and was another way that we could maintain lower prices every day. We didn't need to draw customers into our stores with circulars showing items at special prices; our image of everyday low prices already did that. In addition to the reduced cost of advertising itself, we had further savings at the store level by not having to price and reprice the merchandise with every circular. We were always looking for ways to reduce our costs and pass the savings on to the customer.

In the midnineties, another ingenious idea came from our marketing department and advertising agencies. Why don't we use our own associates instead of professional models in our TV ads and monthly circulars? We tried it. Our associates did a great job, and it was a huge success. The associates who appeared in TV spots and circulars became celebrities in their communities, and Wal-Mart associates from all over the country wanted to be in the commercials.

Our customers noticed the change and loved it. Our marketing department responded once again and came up with the idea of using our customers as models in our ads as well. This was another huge success that made customers associate Wal-Mart as a "people company."

We were also able to tell our customers about our commitment to the environment, about our many Good Works projects, and about our involvement in community activities. We let them know that Wal-Mart is a company for families, and your neighbors are the ones who will be serving you when you come into your local Wal-Mart store. Maybe most importantly, how we present Wal-Mart in our advertising is what customers actually find when they come into our stores. Our marketing has always painted an accurate picture of who we really are and what you can expect when you shop with us.

When Disaster Strikes Your Customers

On May 30, 1982, a tornado devastated Marion, Illinois. It destroyed scores of homes and many businesses. The Wal-Mart store was hit hard as well—the tornado ripped off the back one-third of the building. The people in town were in great need of supplies, not only to live on, but also to clean up the remnants of the devastation. Sam and Jack Shewmaker, the president and COO for Wal-Mart at that time, got in Sam's plane and flew up to assess the situation. When they saw that the town was nearly destroyed and the people had been thrown into dire straits, they first decided to build a temporary wall right where the tornado had cut off the back of our building. They next brought in teams of associates from other Wal-Marts to clean up the store, ordered new merchandise, and reopened within days. They continued to operate the store while the reconstruction of the rear of the building was in process.

The Wal-Mart Way of Enhancing Quality of Life

- A UBS Warburg study found that Wal-Mart grocery prices are 17 to 20 percent lower than other supermarkets, which has the greatest benefit for low-income families.

- According to the New England Consulting Group, Wal-Mart saved consumers $20 billion last year—enough to put a $100 bill in the hands of every adult in America.

- A new Wal-Mart store, Sam's Club, or distribution center in a community means new jobs and lower retail prices in all area stores.

- Wal-Mart generates more than $8 billion in sales tax revenues and millions more in property taxes every year that help to fund such basic services as police, fire, and schools.

One of the greatest problems for communities that experience devastating natural disasters is a shortage of routine and specialized merchandise, which in turn drives up prices. This never happened in Marion. The community's lifeline of everyday supplies flowed without interruption. Many people in the town believed that this was a more significant contribution toward their recovery than any money and goods that Wal-Mart donated.

One year later, the construction was complete, and we had an exciting grand reopening. During that year, with one-third of the store gone, we never had a week when the sales in that store were less than the year before. The customers were amazed at Wal-Mart's efforts, especially Sam's special interest in the project, and they became loyal believers in Wal-Mart. When the rebuilt store opened, the sales skyrocketed and continued to grow at an accelerated rate for years. The customers were grateful for what Wal-Mart did in their time of need and rewarded Wal-Mart with their continued loyalty. When you demonstrate genuine care for people, they care for you.

Thus began a dramatic recovery-response program that is still in operation today. Whenever and wherever a disaster strikes (be it a tornado, hurricane, flood, fire, or anything else), the local Wal-Mart will always be at the front of rescue and recovery efforts. A Disaster Recovery team moves into action and has critically needed merchandise on the way to the scene of the disaster within twenty-four hours. From our experiences, we have developed a list of 150 to 200 items that people desperately need in the immediate aftermath of a disaster: mops, pails, garbage cans and bags, brooms, chain saws, fuel, camp stoves, sleeping bags, bottled water, dog food, baby formula, disposable diapers, and so forth. We do everything we possibly can to expedite getting the right merchandise into the right hands at the right time.

Many of our suppliers participate with us on this and in many cases reduce their cost to us on the most critical items. We pass this cost reduction directly on to our customers, and we even reduce the prices on many other items to help our customers in their time of real need. Frequently, we will bring trailer loads of water into our parking lots and distribute it to people free of charge. If our store is damaged, we work around the clock by bringing in associates from other stores who take shifts in order to reopen it safely as soon as possible. When a local store's recovery is completed so quickly, where do you think the customers in that area are going to do their regular shopping when the crisis is over?

In the Denver, Colorado, area, after that terrible shooting at Columbine High School, students initially couldn't return to their own school and were temporarily transferred to another school. The associates in our Wal-Mart stores in the immediate area decided that since those students couldn't get to their lockers in Columbine and likely needed supplies, they would help. "Why don't we provide them with backpacks, pencils, paper, and whatever other school supplies they might need? For free?"

They went to their store managers with a plan to donate the needed supplies; the managers were happy to be part of the plan. They set up a big tent in the Wal-Mart parking lot to assemble the packages for these high-school students. As a result, all of the Columbine students got their needed supplies when they went back to school—all orchestrated by our associates out there.

Wal-Mart took it one step further when it sent five or six counselors from Resources for Living, at Wal-Mart's expense, to counsel with students and parents in their grief. This is another example of people really caring about other people. In truth, no matter what business you may be in, it's all about people and relationships.

You Are More Important Than a Frying Pan

Customer satisfaction is not a matter of policies and procedures. It is about principles that are written on the hearts of all members of the team so that they know instinctively how to act.

I have my favorite story on customer service. Her story went something like this:

I want to tell you about your store manager in Harlingen, Texas. I want to tell you what he did for me. I was shopping in your store and spent a lot of money. I had a great deal of merchandise, including an electric frying pan. When I loaded my cart, it didn't all fit in so I laid the frying pan at the bottom of my cart. When I went to my car and unloaded all of the bags, I must have forgotten about the frying pan because when I got home, it wasn't in the car. I must have left it on your cart. I called the store and asked a lady there if anyone had turned it in or had found it. I then asked if someone would check in the carts in the parking lot. She said she would get back to me. About fifteen or twenty minutes later, a man called me and said he was the store manager. They had looked all over and hadn't found the frying pan. He asked me to come down and tell him about it and show him what pan she was talking about. He said in the meantime, maybe we will find it. He said, "Just ask for me—my name is Pete Maldonado." I went back to the store and found Maldonado standing right by the front door. He took me over to the frying pan display and asked which one was it. I pointed out to him which one it was, and he handed it to me and said, "Please take this with Wal-Mart's compliments." I said, "Wait a minute. This wasn't your fault, it was my fault. You don't need to do that." He repeated, "Please, take it with Wal-Mart's compliments." So I said to him, "Why would you give me the frying pan when it wasn't even your mistake?" And he said, "You are more important to us than a frying pan."

What an incredible line and what an incredible story. It is also an incredible example of how you cannot put real customer satisfaction in procedures or policies. It is written in someone's heart and mind. It's part of the culture. It's the way we do it here. Maldonado didn't question whether he had the authority to supply the lady with a frying pan. Yes, it would show up as shrinkage on the financial reports for his store, but there was no question about what was the right thing to do. He was going to take care of her no matter what it took, and he did.

The customer wrote a letter to the editor of the local newspaper and it appeared in the paper several days later. That's fantastic—you can't buy that

> *Companies that at their core have a purpose beyond making money, normally end up being the big winners over the long haul. I define purpose as the very definitive difference a company and its people are trying to make in the marketplace. Sam Walton did not put it in these words, but Wal-Mart, in my opinion, was founded and built on the purpose of "democratizing merchandise." With a low cost structure and a fanatical customer focus, Wal-Mart became the great enabler, providing the opportunity for ordinary citizens to buy the same things as rich people. In the process, they have almost single-handedly made the "good life" within reach of most people here and around the world.*
> **—Roy Spence, founder and president, GSD & M Advertising**

kind of advertising. That's better than any ads we could have run on television because it's real. Exceeding customers' expectations is what satisfaction is all about.

Pete Maldonado didn't make an extra sale that day, but he did make a lifelong customer.

Market Research

One of the key methods we used to determine the level of our customers' satisfaction was to have an independent market research firm contact, at random, a percent of the customers in our trade territories and ask them a series of questions about their perceptions of Wal-Mart and our competitors. We did this each month.

We didn't like to hear some of our customers' comments, but they were invaluable in letting us know their true feelings. We studied this survey carefully to determine where we could improve our performance. It allowed us to monitor our progress over time. This became a very valuable tool for us as we grew larger, keeping us in tune with what was really going on at the store level. It's so easy when you become large to rest on your laurels and become complacent. Problems can creep up on you, and you might not even be aware that you are slipping. It is very important to maintain an objective opinion about how well you are executing so you don't fall asleep, as so many companies have.

Many refer to this as "consumer research." At this point I must confess that I really dislike the word *consumer*—almost as much as I dislike the word *boss*. I hear it used so often instead of customer. Consumers are statistics, while customers are people. You can't have a relationship with consumers, but you can with people—and that's what retailing is all about. A key to Wal-Mart's extraordinary success has been the relationships we have built with our customers. I believe it is because they know that we really care about them and their welfare.

For reflection and action:

1. Have you ever experienced great service at a restaurant or store or other place of business? How did it make you feel as a person?

2. Do you ever give serious thought to the quality of service you are providing in your business and community? Have you found effective ways to communicate that these people are important to you?

3. What barriers, if any, stand between you and satisfying your customers? Are you willing to tackle those barriers in order to serve your customers well?

4. How important would your business associates say customer satisfaction is to you? How about your customers?

Chapter 6

A Passion for Excellence

Leadership is the art of accomplishing more than the science of management says is possible.

—Former Secretary of State Colin Powell

Wal-Mart Way Principle #6

Achieving excellence becomes a reality when you set high expectations, humbly face and correct your mistakes, stay optimistic, and avoid the quicksand of complacency.

I joined Wal-Mart Stores in April 1980. Our sales were strong going into the holidays that year, and we had a tremendous selling season between Thanksgiving and Christmas. When I came into the Friday morning meeting the week after Christmas and confirmed that sales had risen nearly 40 percent from the same period in the previous year, I was amazed and extremely excited. I had never seen such a large increase with an established company, especially during what was already the highest sales volume period of the year.

If this had happened anywhere else I had ever worked, it would have been cause for a major celebration. Little did I know that I was about to enter Sam's Wal-Mart Way classroom once again.

Excellence Means "Correction of Errors"

Sam began the meeting by thanking everyone for a great job. We discussed a few of the very positive things that we had done, but after only five minutes of modest self-congratulations, we began discussing what we could have done better. We talked about everything we had "left on the table"—that's when you lose sales due to a lack of merchandise. Sam asked why we had run out of Christmas wrapping paper a week-and-a-half early in some stores. We also discussed overstocking—why we ended up with way too much merchandise in other categories. We spent a full two hours talking about how we could improve our decision making and operations, and we began making specific and detailed plans for the next Christmas season right then. Leadership assigned people to specific tasks and asked them to report back on how they were going to solve some of these problems.

> It is the characteristic excellence of the strong man that he can bring momentous issues to the fore and make a decision about them. The weak are always forced to decide between alternatives they have not chosen themselves.
> —Dietrich Bonhoeffer

This was a profound learning experience for me and introduced me to Sam's simple concept of "correction of errors." This is how we approached every major merchandise season, every company initiative, every major event we were involved in: review everything while it is still fresh in your minds, discover errors, and don't make the same mistake twice. Sam rigorously applied this process to every part of the company and helped us to keep improving everything that we did.

Does this mean we didn't reward and celebrate success? Absolutely not. But Sam didn't see the value of sitting around and talking about how good we were, when there were things we could do better. This was one of my most important lessons on what passion for excellence really looked like.

Passion for Success Means High Expectations

By setting high expectations, we were always raising our performance standards to a new level. That's how we were able to keep improving our numbers from year to year. But the real focus was always on being the best we possibly could be; the numbers would take care of themselves.

One of the keys to setting your expectations high is a spirit of optimism. We had a very optimistic view of America's future, of the business environment, and of ourselves! We believed that there was always more potential than what we and others could see at the moment. That is why we addressed problems and challenges with poise and opportunism. Sam had a positive point of view. Sam was a living example to us of what we could accomplish if we set our minds to it.

Passion for Excellence Means Believing the Impossible Is Possible

High expectations are a powerful driving force, helping you become better than you already are. Sometimes you need to go one step further and step out on faith, even when you don't have history or research to predict success. As the biblical writer said: "Now faith is being sure of what we hope for and certain of what we do not see" (Heb. 11:1). Yes, past performance is the greatest predictor of future performance—but if we lived by that credo alone, no one would do anything bold and new. Sometimes we need good, old-fashioned faith!

Wal-Mart grew 2,000 percent in the seventies and passed the $2 billion mark in 1982. Many retail analysts predicted this as our peak—the more established stores would leave us behind. But that was really only the beginning of the coming Wal-Mart revolution. People continue to be amazed by what we have accomplished in Wal-Mart since that time. And honestly, sometimes in reflecting back on our next period of unbelievable growth, I shake my head and pinch myself to make sure I didn't dream it.

When I joined the company in the first quarter of 1980, Wal-Mart had just completed a year with sales of $1.25 billion, Wal-Mart's first billion-dollar year.

When Sam passed away twelve short years later, in April 1992, our sales had reached $44 billion, making us the largest retailer in the world.

By the end of fiscal year 2004, sales topped $256 billion—an increase of $212 billion over the past twelve years. We had become the largest company in the world. Truth is stranger than fiction, and what I just described to you is impossible. But we did it.

The concept of "impossible" can do funny things to our thinking. We really do limit in our minds what people working together can accomplish in organizations. The extraordinary, the "impossible" things that Wal-Mart accomplished were done by ordinary people. I don't believe that such results are limited to Wal-Mart. I believe there are hundreds and thousands of stories just waiting to be written by organizations and companies who have leaders that inspire people to accomplish things that seem impossible. The only way that can happen, though, is if the leader believes it is possible—has even a mustard seed of faith—and can convince his people that the seemingly impossible is indeed possible.

Passion for Excellence Means Communicating, Communicating, Communicating . . .

Every year we had a different annual theme, which we introduced at the year-beginning meeting held in late January. But our theme didn't fade away when the banner came down; we repeated it over and over again throughout the year. These themes were more than neat little slogans—they were really a focus point to drive home an idea, a rallying point to engage everyone's thoughts. It was an emotional appeal to help us realize we could achieve even higher goals than we had in the past. It was even a way to share our beliefs with everyone in the company—to communicate our culture—and bring everyone in alignment with a high goal. Several examples of the themes for past years are:

We've Only Just Begun!
You Can Do It!
Yes We Can!
Let's Make It Happen!
It's My Wal-Mart!

In 2001, our theme was "Imagine the Possible." Some of us were like little kids getting in trouble for having too-active imaginations. (Usually there was some mischief involved.) All of us have been told in one form or another to get our heads out of the clouds and our feet on the ground. I think to succeed in business and life that there are times when we need do the exact opposite: get our heads back in the clouds and our feet off the ground. In other words, stretch your mind and just imagine, envision, dream of how much better you and your organization can be than you are right now. When was the last time you sent your mind wandering beyond today to imagine a brighter tomorrow? Let your mind go, dream a little, and you might just discover that anything is possible.

Too many leaders are afraid of letting their minds wander too far; they put fences around their dreams. If you want to accomplish great things, you must dare to venture beyond today's realities. The thinking behind "Imagine the Possible" was that we needed to push even further, beyond the self-imposed limits of our current thought processes and previous experiences. My first thought was *Imagine the possible by striving for the impossible*, because that's what we had actually done in the past; why couldn't we do it in the future?

In preparation for my talk to all our store managers about the new theme, I looked the word *impossible* up in dictionary and found the following definition: "Felt to be incapable of being done, attained, or fulfilled."

The key phrase in this definition that jumped off the page to me was "felt to be." There have been many events in history that people perceived to be impossible but then accomplished. Consider:

The Pyramids of Egypt

We still don't know how they were built. How did they get those big rocks on the top levels? Modern engineers still marvel. This was an unbelievable accomplishment for the ancient Egyptian civilization.

Beethoven's Fifth

In 1804, Beethoven completed his Fifth Symphony in spite of the fact that he was completely deaf. He went on to write several other symphonies after losing his hearing. How is it possible to write music when you are deaf? You can't do that—wouldn't you have to know how it sounds? He accomplished what seemed to be impossible.

Breaking the Four-Minute Mile

Track athletes viewed running a mile in under four minutes as impossible. Some doctors believed that it was past the threshold of human potential and would lead to death. Then one day, a young medical student, Roger

Bannister of England, ran a mile in 3:59:4. In the next several years, runners achieved the four-minute mile over three hundred times. Once Bannister broke through the barrier, people believed it could be done—and did it.

The Heart Transplant

When I was growing up, it seemed like science fiction to think that you could take a heart out of one person and transplant it into the body of another. Then, Dr. Christiaan Barnard of South Africa did it. Today, organs are being transplanted hundreds and thousands of times a day all across the world.

Land a Man on the Moon

When I was a child, I read the popular comic strip *Buck Rogers*. Rogers wore a funny-looking outfit and traveled around in space in a shiny rocket. I liked reading *Buck Rogers* because it was like magic—the world of make-believe for young people. But later, the U.S. actually did it: we landed men on the moon and we got them back to Earth. In the 1950s two Harvard scientists conclusively proved that space travel was impossible (because of the weight of the fuel). Today we take space travel for granted.

These achievements were all perceived to be impossible, but they were accomplished. If these things were possible, what else is possible? Are there things in your organization that you or your people may think are impossible that in actuality could be done? No one believed that it was possible to build the largest corporation in the world in Bentonville, Arkansas, but we did it. If you can recognize that what others feel is impossible

> *I know the price of success: dedication, hard work, and an unremitting devotion to the things you want to see happen.*
> —Frank Lloyd Wright

is actually possible, you can open up the boundaries of your mind. Who knows what you may be able to do?

A Passion for Excellence in Wabash, Indiana: A Snapshot

On Monday, October 25, 1999, a fire started in the furniture department on the lamp counter in our Wabash, Indiana, store. The store manager was alerted, and he attempted to extinguish the fire but was unsuccessful. He discovered later that lamp oil on the counter fueled the fire. The fire department arrived and was able to put out the fire fairly quickly. Unfortunately, however, there was extensive smoke damage throughout the store. All of the merchandise had to be removed from the store and salvaged, all of the ceiling tile had to be replaced, and all of the store fixtures had to be cleaned off or repainted.

> *When aligned around shared values and united in a common mission, ordinary people achieve extraordinary results.*
> —Ken Blanchard

In essence, the entire store had to be cleared out and cleaned up before the new merchandise could be brought in and set in place. This was a major undertaking, almost like setting up a whole new store.

The store manager called the executive vice president of operations and said he would have to close the store for approximately twenty-one days. The executive vice president indicated that three weeks was too long for the store to be closed for our customers and challenged the district manager and store-planning vice president to do it in no more than seven days. The race was on.

What did we do?
- Thursday: inventoried the store.
- Friday: shipped all the merchandise out of the store and removed all of the ceiling tile.
- Saturday: cleaned every fixture in the store; painted the store; replaced the carpet and ceiling tile.
- Sunday: received freight.
- Monday: set the merchandise on the counters and opened the store for business at 4 PM.

Some of the most significant achievements during the six days included:
- We built a temporary pharmacy by the front door of the store that operated continuously throughout the crisis.

- The trucking department drove all fourteen thousand ceiling tiles from Oklahoma to Wabash in less than forty-eight hours.

- The store operated a number of departments from tents in the parking lot during the six-day period.

- The Specialty Division reset the photo and jewelry areas in forty-eight hours.

- Company pilots volunteered to help receive and move the merchandise from the back room as it was being unloaded from the company trucks.

- The salvage-company owner said that in his forty-two years in business, he had never seen anything this big accomplished so quickly—that the week should have been submitted for inclusion in the *Guinness Book of World Records*.

- The local K-Mart brought in twenty additional trailers of merchandise into their stores in response to the situation. They thought we would be down for three months. The K-Mart district manager walked around in disbelief when we opened only six days later.

- Store planners drove twelve hours through the first night to get there and guide the setup.

- Carpet layers did a four-day job in eighteen hours.

- Marketing got the store signage to the store from Kansas City in twenty-four hours.

- Merchandising replenished the store from ground zero in less than a week.

- Local warehouses sent a driver to do nothing but move trailers and facilitate the loading and unloading in the store.

- Surrounding Wal-Mart stores sent three hundred associates to help reset the store.

- The local Supercenter fed three hundred workers per day in the parking lot for a week.

- Loss Prevention was on site providing security throughout the entire process, twenty-four hours per day. When the store was inventoried again after the setup, all merchandise was accounted for, and nothing was missing.

And finally, what were the lessons we learned?

- Wal-Mart associates respond to challenges like no other team—it is part of the company culture and gets inside people's thinking. We were vividly reminded that this company and team of people can do anything they put their hearts and minds to.

- Set high goals—get the store up and running in seven days—and then get out of great people's way.

- You can change the way things are done. Who cares if you're supposed to be down for three months or even three weeks?

- Celebrate achievement. The pride the associates showed inspired everyone in Wal-Mart, and management invited key associates in this undertaking to a Saturday meeting to recognize them for their incredible accomplishment.

- It is possible to do the impossible.

The bar had been raised, and every store that has experienced a similar disaster since that time has reopened in less than one week. People from all over the world have called to find out how they did it. This is another example of how the passion for excellence at Wal-Mart has continued to impact industry standards and expectations worldwide.

A Passion for Excellence Means Investing in Your Business

Our Loss Prevention team developed a program that they called Restitution and Civil Recovery, which was a way of getting money back from people who were caught stealing from Wal-Mart. Although our restitution people had done a great job, I knew we weren't reaching our full potential in that area. They had recovered about $2.5 million—about industry standard based on our sales. The $2.5 million was important because it went right to the company's bottom line—ultimately saving our customers money—and was a big increase over the previous year.

The departmental team came in and presented a budget to me for the next year of $3.5 million. They were rightfully proud because percentage-wise, it was a significant increase. I complimented them on their plan to significantly increase recoveries, then asked what it would take to get to $10 million. Their response was, "Ten million? We can't do $10 million. That's not realistic, Don."

I asked them why it wasn't realistic. And they said, "We would have to change everything we do."

I said, "Ah-ha, that's it. So the way you can get the $10 million is by changing what you do? Take a couple of weeks and go back to the drawing board. Come back and tell me what you need in order to get to $10 million in recoveries this year."

The team came back a couple weeks later with their new plan in hand. To achieve 400 percent growth, the plan included adding nineteen people to the home office department, which, of course, was going to add expense before recovering even a single dollar. They went on to say that the plan would also require additional computer programming support in order to get the reports they needed.

I agreed, "Then that's what we'll do. Go ahead and start hiring the nineteen people. I'll talk to the people in information systems, and we'll get the tech support you need to write the programs. If we do that, can I expect you to get the $10 million?"

"Absolutely" was their confident answer.

We added approximately $500,000 dollars of new costs, and in the next twelve months the team reached the $10 million in recoveries. That was a terrific return on our investment. And it was a wonderful example of what happens when the passion for excellence grows throughout a company. They did it; I didn't. It took changing just about everything they did, which wasn't my idea—it was theirs. Yes, leadership challenged them to get their number, but they didn't grumble; they simply accepted the challenge and came back with a solid plan. Yes, they saw that I had a lot of confidence in them and their plan—and I gave them the resources they needed and had clearly defined—but again, they were so excited about blasting through previous achievements that they made it happen.

They did all sorts of fun things to accomplish their goal: contests, colorful wall charts, and their own humorous slogans. It was a joy to watch. The whole department was involved, which created a new measure of enthusiasm and kept the challenging process of working on the recovery of stolen property from being a downer.

At the end of the year we threw a big party for everyone in the department to celebrate their $10 million accomplishment. The next year, they came back with a plan to recover $17 million. Again, they told me exactly what they needed in the way of resources in order to make it happen. They got the $17 million! Not only were they able to do something great for the company, but they also learned—and taught others—the amazing things that can happen with a passion for excellence.

The Loss Prevention team members achieved even more then they ever imagined. They didn't do it—and couldn't have done it—by cutting corners. They accomplished something great by doing their business in a better way and by making an investment in the business.

Business is tough. We are all looking for ways to cut costs. But a passion for excellence is about making wise investments in people and in their ideas.

Passion for Excellence Means Counting the Costs

It's good to set goals above and beyond the status quo. And it's good to dream and believe the impossible is possible. But is there a danger in setting goals that are totally unrealistic and unattainable? Absolutely! When leadership arbitrarily sets goals and hands them off to the team with instructions to "just do it," instead of inspiring people, it has the exact opposite effect: it deflates and demotivates the very people who are responsible for reaching the goals. We all know that without enthusiasm and personal ownership, it is next to impossible to accomplish something significant.

It is vital for a leader to carefully dialogue with people to set goals that stretch them and grow the organization. He or she can push—but the goals must also be achievable and supported with adequate resources. The worst thing a leader can do if people react negatively to an unrealistic goal is ignore their concerns and simply tell them to "do whatever it takes." What too often happens is that the people take the leader at face value and begin cutting corners, which may in turn lead to stretching or reshaping the truth, to the point that good people make bad and possibly illegal or unethical choices.

Any growth achieved in this manner will be short-lived. The costs—loss of trust and damage to company culture—will be much greater.

A Passion for Excellence Means Avoiding the Quicksand of Complacency

Every person I have ever met has wanted to be successful in life. Many of them have managed to reach their goals and have become extremely successful. They have had high expectations for themselves and for their organizations and have accomplished great things. But I have seen a significant number of individuals and companies, which have been very successful for a time, lose it for no apparent reason—at least for no obvious reason. They had continued to have good workers and products and favorable competitive positioning.

> *He who is good at making excuses is seldom good for anything else.*
> —Benjamin Franklin

While it would be easy to overgeneralize and simplify, I have observed that success itself can be a major problem. It can be dangerous to be highly successful. You can begin to think that you have arrived and that you are on top of the mountain. This is when egos inflate in unhealthy ways. Then leaders aren't concerned about the company but begin to say with words and actions, "Look at what I have done!" This can happen in companies and just as easily in individuals.

When our egos get out of control, we lose our humility and become arrogant. We begin to believe that we are always right. Arrogance leads to bad decisions and treating others as second-class citizens. When everyone is patting you on the back and praising your accomplishments, watch out; that's when you are vulnerable.

The ancient Greeks had a word for this: *hubris.* Hubris is an exaggerated pride or self-confidence; an overbearing presumption; arrogance. Unfortunately, the business world is full of stories of great individuals and companies that have fallen due to their own egos. Out-of-control executive perks and indulgences, shady deals meant to appease stockholders, associates who are afraid to question or speak up to leadership: these are just a few of the symptoms of hubris in the business world.

Complacency is the mortal enemy of growth and continued success. It is easy to take success for granted and presume that because we have been successful in the past, success will continue to be our friend in the future. Nothing could be further from the truth. The reality is that you have to work harder the more successful you become—your competitors have learned from your success and are all out to beat you. At Wal-Mart, we always

> *If you love your work, you will be out there every day trying to do it the best you can and soon everyone around you will catch that passion from you—like a fever.*
> —Sam Walton

cautioned our associates not to believe our press clippings. There is always room for improvement. You are never as good as you ultimately can be. As Abraham Lincoln expressed, "I do the very best I know how—the very best I can; and I mean to keep on doing so until the end."

One of the reasons we accomplished so much at Wal-Mart was that we never lost sight of being the best that we could be. We corrected errors, operated with a sense of faith and optimism, set high expectations of ourselves, and guarded against complacency. We celebrated our success but never became enthralled with our own press.

How about you? What great things are ahead for you and your organization when you embrace a passion for excellence?

For reflection and action:
1. Does your company have a passion for excellence? How would you define excellence in your organization?
2. What are some obvious errors that need correcting in your company?
3. Have you ever personally sensed the need to set your sights higher than the level at which you have been performing? What can you do to make that happen?
4. What enemies of excellence exist in your life and company right now?
5. How committed are you to not only doing things right—but the best way they can be done?

Chapter 7

The Execution Imperative

The secret of success is to do common things uncommonly well.
—John D. Rockefeller Sr.

Wal-Mart Way Principle #7

Your success is in direct proportion to your ability to plan, monitor, and ultimately execute all phases of your business.

In *The Wal-Mart Way*, I address a full range of dynamics that must work together to create organizational success. You must start with a compelling vision that is shared throughout the organization and drives all that you do. You must have a product that meets the needs of your customers. You must be able to access resources in capital, assets, and most importantly, great people. You must have well-thought-out strategies that staff implements consistently in order to achieve your objectives. You must reinforce and cultivate an organizational culture that is built on a foundation of sound values and beliefs.

I also share in this book numerous strategies that Wal-Mart gained competency in as integral parts of our success story, including customer satisfaction, respect for our people, merchandising, marketing, pricing, technology, logistics, and community involvement. But the most critical element in any strategy is the ability to actually make it happen; to do it. Wal-Mart's strategies served us only insofar as we executed them to the best of our abilities.

I believe it is possible to have all the right strategies, a fantastic vision, great access to capital, and everything else needed for success but still not ever achieve it. That will always be the case if the people in your company fail to execute. This is where I have seen so many companies fail. How can that be? By the way, how is your organization when it comes to execution?

Attention to Detail

Consistent execution of a company's various programs and strategies is certainly not easy, especially as a company becomes large. There are so many critical decisions and actions that must happen on so many different levels, made by so many different people, and in so many different locations. How does a leader make sure all that happens?

As leaders move higher in an organization and as that organization grows, there is a mistaken assumption, a widespread myth, that they no longer have time to be involved in the details of the business. As it correctly and appropriately becomes necessary for them to delegate more responsibilities and authority to others and to reallocate their time to activities that they consider of higher priority, many leaders make the critical error of losing touch with the frontline people in the organization and with their true boss, the customer.

> *Failure is the opportunity to begin again, more intelligently.*
> —Henry Ford

When leaders lose sight of the details, it is almost impossible for them to effectively evaluate how well their organization is executing. As an additional by-product, I would suggest to you that nothing will demoralize those who work for you more quickly than when you no longer have an active knowledge of what's going on in the business.

There is no question that when people get promoted up the corporate ladder, they can no longer do everything they once did or in the same way they once did it. There simply aren't enough hours in the day. I believe, however, it is essential that to be effective, a leader must continue to find ways to stay in touch with how the company operates.

The first key for a leader to stay intimately involved in the details of the organization is to have a system in place that allows him or her to monitor details at a glance. We live in an information age, and with all the reports and sortable data that is instantly available at any manager's fingertips, it is amazing how many leaders allow reports to stack up and gather dust on a corner of their credenzas. I'm not calling for more reports. But do read the ones you have.

The second key for leaders to stay intimately involved in the details of their organizations is to get out of their offices and head to where the action is. Work beside someone for a couple of hours. Ask him questions about his job. Talk to customers. (I will cover this in more detail later in the chapter.)

We have heard in recent years about too many senior leaders denying any responsibility for significant wrongdoing in their organizations because they weren't aware of what was happening. While it is true that no organization is immune to individual managers and supervisors making bad and unethical decisions on key strategic issues, leadership must find a way to stay informed.

I do not believe that there is one right way for a leader to stay involved; the very nature of a particular business will dictate what is and what is not possible, and what is most important. But the key is for the leader to find a way to continue to receive feedback, both formally and informally, in order to effectively judge what's going on.

Leaders Must Stay in Touch

Effective communication within an organization takes hard work. To stay in touch, you must remove physical distance as a barrier to be sure that your communication is not being filtered through too many layers. You must find a way to remain close to your associates and customers, making sure that you are available and not living in an ivory tower. Long before it became a popular business acronym, Sam believed in MBWA (management by walking around). Apart from all the good intentions and principles of providing outstanding customer satisfaction, there must be a method of evaluating the actual execution of those intentions and principles. You have to be sure that what you think should happen is actually taking place. We did it several ways.

Constant In-Store Presence

First of all, we established a structure that kept leadership in constant contact with associates and customers. In Wal-Mart or any large retail chain, with stores and clubs scattered across large geographic areas, you obviously can't be aware of everything that goes on everywhere at every moment, but that doesn't mean you don't try.

In Wal-Mart, from the beginning, every store manager reported to a district manager who supervised six to twelve stores, depending on the size of the stores and the geography. The district manager lived in close proximity to those stores and spent time in each one at least once every two weeks, helping the management team and associates to improve their store. Their chief responsibility was to see that the Wal-Mart programs—including people programs for our associates—were being executed effectively. No wonder programs such as the Open Door worked. Associates got to know the district manager by name and could count on seeing him or her on a regular basis.

Each district manager reported to a regional vice president who supervised approximately ten district managers and one hundred stores. The regional vice presidents lived in northwest Arkansas and flew out to their stores every Monday morning on a Wal-Mart plane and returned home every Thursday evening. They visited every one of their stores approximately every three months. In addition to visiting Wal-Mart stores, they also visited our competitors' stores, This centralized structure provided experienced eyes examining the entire retail landscape every single day. We observed what we were doing well, what we were doing poorly, and what others were doing better than we were. Management made improvements store by store on all of these trips.

Senior Leaders in the Field

In addition to the constant contact of the district managers and regional vice presidents, Sam was personally in numerous Wal-Mart stores every week. He went into the office around 4:00 or 5:00 AM to do some paperwork and reply to letters he had received. He then headed for the airport and flew out to get a firsthand look at how the stores were performing and looked, how the associates were doing, and how we were serving our customers. He also provided a lot of inspiration to the associates in the stores, and they loved him. He thanked them for the way their stores looked and for their efforts, and he reminded them of how important it was to satisfy the customers.

Sam also insisted that every senior officer travel to several Wal-Mart stores at least one day every week. We flew out early in the morning on one of the company planes to both large and small markets, visiting up to five or six stores in a day. At the end of a long and productive day, we either flew home that night or stayed the course for a second or third day of visits. We all headed in different directions so we could get senior leadership into as many stores as possible. We checked the merchandise, checked the condition of the store, visited with as many associates as we could, visited with the customers, shared our detailed observations with the store management team, usually stopped at a competitor's store to see what we could learn from them, then went to the airport to fly to the next store.

While in each store, we asked the customers what they liked and what they didn't like about our store. You know what? They were very honest with us. We also asked our associates how things were going in the store and how the in-store management team was treating them. Sometimes they were reluctant to say anything, but

> *If you see a snake, just kill it. Don't appoint a committee on snakes.*
> —H. Ross Perot

most of the time they called it like it was. We always attempted to be accessible to anyone who wanted to visit with us, however, it was impossible to help people with problems if they weren't willing to come forward and share their concerns.

If the store was having problems, that was usually very apparent, and frequently we could provide assistance while we were there. If a store was really operating badly, we might stay there all day and not visit any other stores. As I look back on it now, those were special times for me. I loved visiting with the associates—they're great people! When traveling today, even though I have retired from the company, I still stop by Wal-Marts just to speak with the associates.

There is no question in my mind that these visits were powerful in keeping the small-company feeling alive no matter how large we became. By visiting our stores religiously, we were able to share and reinforce our values and culture and to communicate to our associates how valuable they were to our continued success and how critical it was to take extremely good care of our customers. We

> *A person who is successful has simply formed the habit of doing things that unsuccessful people will not do.*
>
> **—Anonymous**

worked hard to make sure our executive team was accessible. We were ordinary people, and we genuinely cared about them as individuals.

The Wal-Mart aviation department really made the centralized structure work by getting the regional vice presidents, senior leaders, and other home office associates out to the field on a timely basis. Pilots usually dropped us off at small airports that were very near our stores, enabling us to spend a maximum amount of time making our rounds. We also needed a good way to get our buyers out to the field. They, too, traveled whenever possible to talk with department managers and customers about their lines of merchandise, to see how they were displayed and how well they were selling. We called this "Eat what you cook." We wanted our buyers to experience the same thing as their customers in the store environment. The aviation department made all of this possible.

Think about the travel and time expense of getting our management team into the field. You may be wondering how we could afford such a commitment of resources. We came to understand we could not afford any less commitment than our best!

Sam understood and often quoted a very simple management principle: "Retail is detail."

Some detail-oriented management meetings were another way we stayed in touch with how the company was operating.

The Friday Management Meeting

Every Friday morning, the regional vice presidents attended a management meeting that included all company officers and division heads. During this time, leadership members discussed all aspects of that week's business. They brought to the table any problems they observed during the week in any area of the business; they made decisions and set plans. Anyone in the meeting could share—and was expected to share—any pertinent information about his or her area of the business. To some leaders this might seem a little intimidating and too time consuming, but in Wal-Mart, this was a vital way for us to stay on top of execution.

The discussion was very candid and open. No holds were barred, and we got to the heart of an issue. Occasionally people's feelings got hurt. We tried not to get personal, but sometimes people crossed lines—and made appropriate apologies! We tried to put all issues on the table, realizing if we didn't thoroughly understand a problem, we would never be able to solve it. We expected the appropriate people to develop solutions and report back to the group by the next

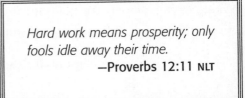

Hard work means prosperity; only fools idle away their time.
—Proverbs 12:11 NLT

meeting, if not sooner. This meeting was crucial in helping senior leaders and all division heads stay close to every function of the business and provided the opportunity to ask questions about anything that wasn't perfectly clear. It was also an ongoing challenge to the quality of our execution.

Merchandise and Operations Meeting

At noon, the regional vice presidents then met with the buyers and together discussed what they had just seen in the stores and clubs from a merchandise standpoint that week. With the regional VPs fresh from the Friday management meeting, they could bring the entire buying division in touch with what was going on in the field and had the opportunity to share merchandising issues with the field operations. Senior leaders frequently attended and participated in this meeting as well. These meetings were not always fun—many debated differences of opinion, sometimes with strong feelings. The purpose of these meetings was not only to share information but also to solve problems, resolve differences of opinion, agree on solutions, and then go out and make it happen.

Profit-and-Loss Review

Once a month, we held a profit-and-loss review meeting within the regular Friday morning meeting. We examined the P&L in detail—and as you already anticipated, no holds were barred. Everyone had to come prepared. We reviewed even small items such as postage or phone charges, and we gave each item close scrutiny. All leaders were expected to be able to answer questions about any of their departments' numbers that were not on budget. This kind of accountability forced everyone to analyze his or her numbers very carefully and take corrective action immediately. Constant monitoring of expenses at all levels helped to keep our costs in line and kept us from having any big quarterly or year-end surprises to report to stockholders. Everyone was involved in expense control all the time.

Informal Feedback

If you want to be an effective leader, you need to cultivate one-on-one feedback from trusted individuals throughout your organization, touching all the different levels. Not people who will tell you what you want to hear, but what you need to hear.

> *Success, real success, in any endeavor demands more from an individual than most people are willing to offer—not more than they are capable of offering.*
> —James Roche

Over time, I developed relationships with a number of store managers, district managers, distribution managers, regional vice presidents, and longtime hourly associates whose opinions I respected. I knew I could trust them to tell me exactly what they thought. I frequently called them and found out how they felt things were going, how the associates' morale was, and what their biggest concerns were. This was a great way for me to stay in touch and keep my finger on the pulse of the company. There were times when I didn't like what I heard, but the input was frequently helpful in determining action that we needed to take.

I also called to ask their opinions if we were planning a major change in a program. These associates were ones who really loved the company and therefore didn't just tell me what they thought I wanted to hear. Instead, they thought about it and gave me great feedback on exactly what they thought the impact would be on associates, customers, and the overall company.

I believe that these informal relationships can be valuable to senior leaders as long as they use the information they receive in a confidential way. It is also a great encouragement to these associates to know that their opinions are important to you, and that they can make a significant difference in the company. This is another way to help your people understand that leadership cares about them.

Associate Access to Senior Leadership

The doors to the executive offices were always open unless we had a private meeting with someone. The physically open door was a symbol: senior leadership was accessible to our associates. Associates always knew they could walk into our offices anytime they wanted to and share with us an idea that they had come up with or something that concerned them. We always listened to our associates.

Another important way to stay informed was through what I described in chapter 4, the Open Door. More than just a means of voicing complaints, the Open Door was a useful way to hear what was on our associates' minds and listen to their suggestions for improving the company. And we didn't just wait for associates to come to us. The open door swung both ways. Our leaders practiced MBWA in the home office in the same way they did in the field. I still have people tell me how much they appreciated the access they had to us and the opportunity we gave them to share their ideas in an informal way and be themselves.

As you can see, Wal-Mart places a great deal of emphasis on communication and staying in touch with the ground-level functioning of the company. At the same time, I realize that this does not assure that everything will be done perfectly. Wal-Mart, like every other company, is made up of imperfect people, and sometimes leaders make mistakes. But our leaders make every effort to be aware of what's going on so that we can head off problems and continue to improve. In order to accomplish this, leadership works extremely hard at paying attention to the details of the business.

Everyday Low Costs—the Productivity Loop

"If I've learned anything about Wal-Mart, it's that cost is king," said Edward Fox, director of the J. C. Penney Center for Retail Excellence at Southern Methodist University. He continued, "They have an almost single-minded focus on reducing costs. It's imbued throughout the organization. They are very stingy when they buy for America and distribute products for America."[1]

There is no argument that everyday low prices stand out as a significant reason customers shop at Wal-Mart. And everyday low prices are not possible without everyday low costs. Since the day I joined Wal-Mart, I never questioned the company's strong emphasis on keeping costs as low as possible and finding ways to reduce them even further.

> *Every time we save a dollar, that puts us one more step ahead of the competition—which is where we always want to be.*
> —Sam Walton

To fully understand the Wal-Mart strategy on controlling costs in order to reduce prices to customers, you must understand the logic behind it. The principle at the heart of making this work was what we called the Productivity Loop.

The Productivity Loop says that if you can drive costs out of the business, you can reduce prices to your customers. If you reduce prices to your customers, your sales should increase. When your sales increase, your costs as a percent of sales go down, making it possible to reduce your prices to

Increase Sales   **Reduce Costs**

**Reduce
Retail
Prices**

customers again, and so on. Add to that formula a constant cultural pressure to reduce all other unnecessary costs in the business, and it is possible to achieve a compounding effect. Although it's really quite a simple formula, many people didn't believe that we could continue to make it work. But the Productivity Loop method and philosophy are still working today, and we keep reducing prices to the customer.

Driving Costs Out

The only way to continue to reduce costs is to make it a priority and weave that philosophy into the very fabric of the culture of the organization. It also requires the leaders' diligence and discipline and demands accountability for all costs, no matter how large or small. That's a hallmark of the Wal-Mart way of doing business: driving unnecessary costs out of every area. It is a relentless pursuit of finding ways to do it better, improving productivity and passing savings on to the customer.

There are many possible approaches to attacking costs in an organization, but one thing I know for certain: you must attack them constantly or they will grow disproportionate to your sales, and as a result, your profits will be in jeopardy. The steps necessary for an effective expense control program in any organization are:

- Create a company-wide consciousness about controlling all expenses.
- Carefully watch what you spend.
- Maintain a discipline about how you spend it.
- Periodically review your processes.
- Simplify the processes that you can.
- Eliminate what you don't need (including entire functions).
- Consolidate functions that make sense.
- Improve productivity with the help of systems and automation.
- Establish accountability throughout the organization.

Since everyday low costs were essential to our overall marketing strategy, cost control had to be ingrained into our daily lives at Wal-Mart. We believed that we needed to have policies that reinforced this same attitude. We believed that we needed to pay attention to the details of the business and be very diligent in analyzing all of our numbers constantly to spot any developing problems. Finally, we believed that we needed to stop every once in a while and reexamine everything we did and look for opportunities to change and improve.

Following are excerpts from an article by Bradford C. Johnson, a consultant with the business research group, McKinsey Company.

Retail may be the last place you would expect to find a productivity miracle. Yet retail productivity growth, as measured by real value added per hour, jumped from 2 percent (1987–95) to 6.3 percent (1995–99), explaining nearly one quarter of the economy-wide acceleration in productivity. More than half of the productivity acceleration in the retailing of general merchandise can be explained by only two syllables: Wal-Mart. A variety of Wal-Mart innovations, both large and small, are now industry standards. Wal-Mart created the large-scale, or "big-box," format; "everyday low prices"; electronic data interchange (EDI) with suppliers; and the strategy of expanding around central distribution centers. These innovations allowed the company to pass its saving on to customers. The Wal-Mart story is a clear refutation of new-economy hype. At least half of Wal-Mart's productivity edge stems from managerial innovations that improve the efficiency of stores and have nothing to do with IT [information technologies]; employees who have been cross-trained, for instance, can function effectively in more than one department at a time. Better training of cashiers and monitoring of utilization can increase productivity rates at checkout counters by 10 to 20 percent. Competitors began to adopt Wal-Mart's innovations in earnest in the mid-1990s. Wal-Mart still has a large productivity edge over its competitors and continues to raise the bar.[2]

There are numerous examples of the way we kept costs down on a day-to-day basis. We chose not spend a lot of money on fancy offices and found that they worked just as well as the finest offices in the country. Our home office is very modest. In fact, a number of years ago, a stock analyst referred to our offices as looking like an "early bus station." A major portion of the office space is converted warehouse space.

> *People of mediocre ability sometimes achieve outstanding success because they don't know when to quit. Most men succeed because they are determined to.*
> —George Herbert Allen

It is an open office layout with small modular offices outfitted with very plain but functional office furniture. Executive offices are also very small, but functional. We never had to explain to store associates who visited the home office why we had such elaborate offices while we were asking them to keep costs down in the stores and clubs. We spent our dollars where they counted most: in the stores and clubs and for our customers.

Some representatives from McDonald's corporate office showed me a video many years ago. They had interspersed excerpts of speeches given by Sam Walton and Ray Kroc, the legendary geniuses responsible for the development of their fine companies. They did it to demonstrate how similar Sam and Ray were in their approaches to business. Mr. Kroc said in this speech to his people, "We should never forget how we did it when we were poor." When I heard that, it hit me how important it is to remember how we got where we are and to never forget what it took. One of the important reasons that Wal-Mart achieved what it did was by controlling costs.

Two to a Room

For newcomers to the Wal-Mart management team, perhaps the first cultural hurdle is embracing our travel policy. When the business requires travel, each associate shares a motel room with another Wal-Mart manager of the same gender. Oh, and don't plan on staying at the Four Seasons; it's more likely to be the La Quinta Inn or Motel 6. They have nice, clean rooms and are moderately priced.

It is important to have good, healthy meals while you travel, but we didn't feel that extravagant meals in five-star restaurants or hotels was a good return on investment. If you choose to order alcoholic beverages after work, you do so at your expense. At the same time, you can't have suppliers pay for your meals; always go Dutch treat.

If you fly commercial airlines, you book your ticket in advance to get the maximum discount. If an emergency comes up and you must book a ticket less than seven days before departure, an executive vice president has to approve the fare. No first-class seats, only coach. Frequent-flyer miles? They stay with the company and help defray the cost of future business trips. All those cost savings get plowed into price savings for our customers, and that's what makes it all worthwhile.

Two to a room, though, has a more important place in Wal-Mart culture than just cutting costs. In many respects two to a room is a blending of several important elements in our culture. The emphasis on costs is obvious. Probably less obvious is the one-on-one communication opportunities it provides. It was a very valuable way for associates, even officers, to share ideas, talk about the business, and learn from each other. As Sam Dunn, the vice president and CFO of Sam's Club, recently shared with me:

> *Over the years, I have traveled and bunked with many other associates. Many of them were really talented individuals and I gleaned from them business principles and cultural values as we philosophized, shared ideas, and compared*

notes before retiring for the night or tuning in a good ball game from the understated comfort of our La Quinta double beds. The experience of rooming with Rob Walton, our chairman of the board, at a midpriced hotel in Mexico City in 1992 was a real eye-opener. We were there to meet with our joint venture partners, Cifra, as we launched our first Sam's Clubs in Mexico. I was a young finance director with just a few years' experience. Sam Walton had only recently passed away and his oldest son, Rob, had taken on the chairmanship and the responsibility of turning Wal-Mart into a global enterprise. Mexico was our first international effort. On this particular trip, several key executives accompanied us, but I somehow ended up sharing a hotel room with Rob. It so happened that Rob was training for his second Ironman Triathlon, and I was an avid runner. We got up in the mornings at 5 AM and ran from our hotel to Chapultepec Park and back, had breakfast together, and spent our days in meeting on a growth strategy for Mexico. Imagine what it meant that the chairman of the board would hang out after business hours and exchange ideas with a young, developing director!

The Power of a Symbol

"Two to a room" is a symbol of our cost consciousness. It is constant reminder to our associates when they travel that they must watch their expenses in everything they do.

I believe that symbols are a very important way of teaching principles. Symbols can present a mental picture of an important idea or concept. The yellow smiley face that we use a great deal in Wal-Mart promotion is an example of how we all should look. It is a reminder of friendliness and treating others with kindness and respect. Another example of a meaningful symbol is the Wal-Mart cheer. People outside the company don't understand the relevance of a cheer in a business—it sounds like high school stuff. The cheer, however, is a way of having a little fun and at the same time bringing everyone together in a form of celebrating our company. It signifies unity and helps us to begin each day and each meeting on a happy note.

We use many other symbols of cultural issues at Wal-Mart, including the modest office decor, the people-greeters, the posting of the Wal-Mart stock price in the home office and every store and club every day, and many other things big and small. I believe that many leaders underuse symbols as a tool that offers a wonderful opportunity to reinforce the culture of any organization.

The Dangers of Bureaucracy

As a business grows larger, it is even more important to control costs, but at the same time, it gets harder. The further the leadership gets away from the details of the operations, the greater the chance for slippage. Unnecessary costs creep into a business in many ways. Everyone needs an assistant, the assistants need assistants, and instead of managers being generalists, they call for more specialists. At this point, the bureaucracy has arrived. We install computers to reduce the clerical work but don't reduce the payroll accordingly—we need people to read and interpret the myriad of reports. We grow larger, and the bureaucracy grows faster than the sales. The bureaucrats add to the workload by developing new reports that everyone needs to receive. The list of people who receive reports becomes endless. Before long, the bureaucracy is full-blown and costing the company money.

Bureaucrats not only add to the payroll and create additional work, but they also stifle innovation and initiative so that it takes longer to get things done. A U.S. congressman spoke at a Saturday morning meeting many years ago and shared his view on bureaucrats. He compared bureaucrats to cockroaches. He said that "it isn't what they eat that's the problem, it's what they get into and mess up that's the real concern."

Bureaucracy is clearly a danger to the cost structure of any organization. At Wal-Mart, it was a constant battle to keep bureaucracy from growing. Management carefully scrutinized all departmental expenses monthly and challenged all recommended changes in structure. Periodically, we called for a moratorium on hiring any additional people and a reassessment of staffing in each department to determine what work could be eliminated. A basic principle that we followed was that you can't reduce costs without eliminating the work. It's really remarkable how many expenses are unnecessary and how much waste can build up in any organization over time. We found that even with constant diligence, periodic soul-searching was essential.

Continuing to keep pressure on costs in every area requires constant discipline because they slip in from everywhere. In order to maintain that discipline, a leader must pay attention to details, keep in touch with people, and continually monitor execution at all levels.

Throughout this book, the subject of culture keeps coming up. It is inevitable. I can't share the Wal-Mart success story with you without the constant reminder that at the heart of everything we have done is this special

> *Genuine success does not come from proclaiming our values, but from consistently putting them into daily action.*
>
> **—Ken Blanchard**

and unique culture. Without a firm conviction over the years in senior leadership to maintain and strengthen that culture, there is no doubt in my mind that we could never have accomplished what we have.

I strongly believe that any individual and any organization are capable of doing the impossible, if they choose to. At the same time, I believe that it won't just happen by itself. I only wish that all leaders could understand the incredible impact that a carefully thought-out and consistently demonstrated culture can have on the results of their organization. I'm talking about a culture rooted in sound core values, totally focused on the customer as the reason for being in business, and recognizing the importance of treating their people with the respect and dignity that they deserve.

Sam's Eagle Eye

Shortly after I retired, I received this e-mail from Harry Jordan, a Wal-Mart buyer. He describes, very effectively, how seemingly little things can impact the performance of a large company on a continuing basis and how the culture is preserved from one generation to another.

Dear Don,

I read a story today in the Arkansas Democrat-Gazette newspaper on a recent speech you made to a business group in Little Rock. Your topic concerning Mr. Sam's "Eagle Eye" for detail brought back an experience I feel compelled to share. The memory that came to mind occurred a few years ago while I was working as a Wal-Mart Buyer in the Automotive Electronics category. I happened to be in the modular layout room one day when your assistant somehow tracked me down by phone and asked, "Do you have a few minutes to come see Don this afternoon?" The thought that a person at your level of responsibility in a company as large as ours was calling me directly was frankly both thrilling and scary! As I jumped into my car and sped to the home office my mind raced with anticipation; was it my sales? My inventory? A supplier or store issue? What was so important that "Mr. Soderquist" would take the time to ask to see me personally? As I sat down in front of your desk after a cordial greeting, you might remember that you held up the package for one of my items and the conversation went something like this: "Harry, I bought this radar detector cord the other day. The directions on the package say 'refer to Figure B'—well, can you show me where 'Figure B' is?"

I was stunned, not by the fact I made a mistake by not proofing my supplier's packaging better, but because you cared enough to take the time to personally point this out. You were deeply concerned that it would be very confusing to a customer. This incredible attention to detail and the will to follow through and take action not only impacted me, but has been a real-life "teaching parable" that I've repeated many times since. Young buyers and new suppliers understand our unique culture better when they hear this story as an example of how everyone from the top down strives to understand the details of our business. Though I never had the privilege of seeing Mr.

My success just evolved from working hard at the business at hand each day.

—Johnny Carson

Sam's passion for questioning the details in person, I want to thank you for serving as a personal example that I can share with others as we expand the Wal-Mart culture.

For reflection and action:

1. Is your organization known for its follow-through and execution?

2. Do you inspect what you expect?

3. How aware are you of the various details that make your business work?

4. In your personal life, what are some ways you can improve on your follow-through and execution?

Chapter 8

Technology—the Ultimate Change Agent

Give me six hours to chop down a tree and I will spend the first four sharpening the axe.

—Abraham Lincoln

Wal-Mart Way Principle #8

To build a great company, you must actively and continually seek out, evaluate, and invest in the tools that best serve the people and aims of your organization.

It is the responsibility of every leader to maximize the contribution of every asset in the business. Generally, only a few of those assets have the potential to be significant drivers in the business and facilitate change throughout the enterprise. Technology and logistics (which I will discuss in the next chapter) are two such resources that have had a dramatic impact on the performance of Wal-Mart. They also represent the principle of teamwork between functional units in a business and the synergy that can result. While numerous articles have been written about Wal-Mart's technology, few people recognize the significant role it has played in supporting the company's total operation.

It would be wrong to begin this chapter without first talking about our associates in relation to technology. You may have noticed that Wal-Mart associates and Wal-Mart culture are the continuing themes woven throughout this book. From the beginning of our testing and use of computers, Sam insisted that all of our systems be people-supportive, not the other way around. Our goal has been to literally put the power of the computer into the hands of our associates in order to make their work more productive and to help them make well-informed decisions.

Technology is only a tool and is not as important as people, but it is a powerful resource that is available to every business, regardless of size, and can have a major impact on a company's sales, profitability, and overall success. It can help to control expenses, provide valuable information on every aspect of a business, aid in the decision-making process, reduce the time needed to accomplish tasks, improve customer service, and maximize the use of other assets. There are four requirements that are essential to ensure that a company receives the maximum benefit that technology can provide:

> *He that will not apply new remedies must expect new evils.*
> —Francis Bacon

1. Senior leadership involvement and support.
2. Selection of the right person to lead the technology department.
3. Investment in the right projects.
4. A method of determining actual payback.

Making Technology Pay

Wal-Mart has always placed a great deal of emphasis on the effective use of technology and considered it an investment rather than an expense. As a

> *We don't want to be famous for our technology.*
> *We want to be famous for what our technology allows us to do.*
> —Linda Dillman, EVP & CIO, Wal-Mart Stores, Inc.

result, we always expected a payback on that investment just as with any other investment we made. I confess that there were times when some questioned the size of our technology investment, but, in retrospect, this investment has proven to be one of the more significant factors in our success.

Technology has been an enabler and facilitator of change throughout

Wal-Mart. It has made it possible for us to dramatically change not only the way we do business, but also the way business is conducted in the entire industry. As a result of the support of senior leadership, Wal-Mart has consistently been on the leading edge of practical technological breakthroughs in equipment, software, and communications technology, a proactive approach that has kept us far ahead of all competitors in taking advantage of the opportunities that technology affords.

Sam's Early Fascination with Computers

In his early days in the retail business, Sam was intrigued by the potential of computers and how he could use them to improve his business. The day I met him, he was visiting with Ben Franklin executives about the possibility of franchising discount stores in small rural communities. It was 1963, and he had already opened his first version of a discount store in Rogers, Arkansas.

I was the data-processing manager (that's what they called technology back then) at Ben Franklin Stores. He spent an entire afternoon with me asking probing, insightful, and far-reaching questions about what computers were capable of doing now and my opinion about how they could be used in the future to manage a business more effectively. He was incredibly inquisitive and took notes the entire time. After I got to know him, I realized that was just a part of who he was—that he never stopped learning and looking for ways to improve all areas of the business. Never.

What has amazed me as I have looked back at that experience was that Sam seemed to have almost a sixth sense that technology would someday have a major impact on business. You have to remember that in 1963 no one could have conceived that computers would become so powerful and so cost-effective that they would be driving major business functions. Sam, a small-town business entrepreneur who began with the dream of owning his own store, was at the forefront of the practical application of this important business tool.

I have noted numerous times in this book that Sam hired for attitude as much as he hired for ability. This included his filling of positions at executive levels, which, as I've mentioned, were almost always in-house promotions.

> *Progress is a tide. If we stand still we will surely be drowned. To stay on the crest, we have to keep moving.*
>
> —Harold Mayfield

In emphasizing Sam's insistence on personal character and presentation among Wal-Mart associates, I don't want to give the misleading impression that he was not highly driven by competence. He not only wanted things done right; he wanted things done best. I believe that is why he was so far ahead of the retail industry in looking for, testing, and adopting the use of cutting-edge technology.

Senior Leadership Involvement

When I joined the Wal-Mart leadership team, we observed that in many companies, the senior leadership members were not involved in systems development—they just let the technicians decide what systems to develop and institute. Why? New technology, almost by definition, is not easy to understand. It is much easier for leaders to delegate the task of staying on top of technological developments to specialists than do the hard work of asking questions and participating in the steep learning curve. No wonder there was a concurrent natural tendency for technical people, who were highly compartmentalized in those days, to be captivated by the systems side of the business but not have an understanding of the real needs of the company.

We always focused our technological efforts on the areas of the business where they could make the greatest impact. We focused, therefore, on the automation of store operations—anywhere we could improve service to our stores and therefore to our customers. It was the responsibility of the operating departments to determine what the systems priorities for their department were. I'm sure this was very frustrating to many seasoned department managers, who already knew how things were supposed to be done and knew how to make things happen. Why fix something that isn't broken? Who knows if this computer stuff will work anyway? But determining systems priorities was in their job description, so they did it.

Next, the operating departments partnered with the technology department to develop a basic design of a system and calculate the anticipated payback. Several times a year, senior leadership reviewed and approved these priorities and estimated paybacks.

After the system was completed and implemented, the operating department compared the payback to the original estimate to insure that they were achieving the results anticipated and, if not, assess why. Based on that analysis, the department determined if any refinements were needed. As a matter of practice, we

> *One machine can do the work of fifty ordinary men. No machine can do the work of one extraordinary man.*
> —Elbert Hubbard

continuously made refinements to existing systems. As we developed new insights, we incorporated these ideas in order to improve the overall system.

Systems Associates as Business Leaders

We believed it was important for the information-systems associates to be business leaders, not merely technicians. The executive responsible for technology was a member of the senior leadership team of the company— to my knowledge, we were the first major retailer to place someone at this level—who participated in all of our meetings and stayed involved in all major business initiatives. The involvement and input from our tech staff on the front lines was extremely valuable in the decision-making process in areas where systems support would be needed. We were so fortunate, over the years, to have leadership in technology that was not only highly competent in the technical side but who also zealously focused on the needs of the business. Our information-systems associates have all been visionaries who anticipated the increasing growth of the business and prepared for the needs of tomorrow.

They also had an unusual and contagious sense of urgency in what they did, often causing the members of their entire department to think and act with the same intensity. Anytime someone brought up a problem or issue related to technology in a meeting, it was not uncommon to see one of the systems associates get up and leave the meeting hurriedly, only to reappear before the meeting was over with either an answer or a commitment to find an answer before next week.

The systems associates developed systems by actually working in the areas that they were assigned, interacting directly with the people who would have to make the systems work. They were assigned to a specific functional team, which allowed them to get a full understanding of the workings of that area, not just the technical side. And at least once a year, usually during the Christmas season when the stores were extremely busy, systems associates did something we called

> Companies should strive to provide the individualized customer service of the old days, while embracing the technology of the future.

Store (or Club) Appreciation, where nearly all of the systems associates went out and worked in the stores and clubs, doing what the store associates had to do. This was a great education for them, and they learned about the practical application of the systems they developed.

The commitments of Wal-Mart's Information Systems Division were:

1. Know the Business.
2. Build It Right.
3. Show the Value.
4. Count on Us.
5. Teach Them.

At Wal-Mart, these five commitments were based on and underscored by the simple motto: "Think like a merchant." Admittedly, this is an unusual statement for a technology department, but that's how Wal-Mart's technology workers stayed attuned to the needs and realities of our business. Information-systems workers tend to be bright, resourceful, and creative. I think that simple motto, "Think like a merchant," is what made our information-systems associates the very best in the business.

Leading the Way

In addition to their detailed involvement in our business, our information-systems associates also have outstanding technical skills. Wal-Mart has been at the forefront of almost all technological innovation in the retail industry. We were one of the first retailers to effectively use electronic scanners for point-of-sale (POS) capture of item movement at the cash register.

We were leaders in the development of the Universal Product Code (UPC) and its placement on all merchandise, a process in which the manufacturer assigns a unique but standardized code to each individual item. This method has revolutionized order processing, scanning customers' merchandise at the front registers, data collection, replenishment, and other aspects of business for every retailer and every manufacturer in the world. The retailing industry did not generally accept UPC in its early days. Many thought it would be impossible to get everyone to agree on standardization and that the method would ultimately cost too much for everyone to adopt. Our perseverance prevailed, though, and we made it happen. Today, nearly every retailer and manufacturer in the world uses UPC and recognizes it as the very foundation of all merchandise processing.

Wal-Mart was also the first retailer to extensively use Electronic Data Interchange (EDI) for transmission of purchase orders for merchandise directly to manufacturers, then receive their confirmation and invoices back from them electronically. This process has considerably reduced time, errors, and costs for the entire industry.

We've never shied away from a technological advance if it would help us fulfill the Wal-Mart vision. To quote once again from Bradford C. Johnson in the McKinsey Quarterly:

> The company [Wal-Mart] invested in most of the waves of retail IT systems earlier and more aggressively than did its competitors; it was among the first retailers to use computers to track inventory (1969), just as it was one of the first to adopt bar codes (1980), EDI for better coordination with suppliers

(1985), and wireless scanning guns (late 1980s). These investments, which allowed Wal-Mart to reduce its inventory significantly and to reap savings, boosted its capital productivity and labor productivity. Wal-Mart's secret was to focus its IT investments on applications that directly enhanced its core value proposition of low prices. The company's later IT investments—such as the Retail Link program, which captures sales data and gives vendors real-time stock and flow information—are aimed more at increasing sales through micro-merchandising and cutting the incidence of stock-outs.[1]

We've consistently been among the first in the retail industry when it comes to finding and creating new opportunities through technology. In 1987, Wal-Mart developed a satellite communications network that extended to every store, every club, and every distribution center in the country. We used the network to transmit the stores' merchandise orders directly into our main computer for processing. After processing, the order-filling documents were sent to the specific distribution center that evening for filling and shipping the next day. Simultaneously, the computer adjusted and maintained the store inventories for every item in the store.

Later on, we used the satellite network to speed up credit-card approval and transactions for the stores and clubs. We also used this system for many other types of communication, including transmission of training programs to the stores and clubs as well as messages from senior management directly to the associates in the field.

Currently, Wal-Mart is leading the way once again. ISD is at the forefront of encouraging the retail industry to invest in radio-frequency identification (RFID) as a means of better identifying and controlling the flow of freight through the entire supply chain. As a benefit to both retailer and supplier alike, RFID literally opens a whole new window to the supply chain that makes it possible to identify and trace the exact location of every single carton of freight and what's in that particular carton at any moment in time. It makes it possible to inventory an entire store electronically and accurately without having to count the merchandise. I am convinced that RFID, too, will become a major breakthrough technology in the years ahead. And Wal-Mart is out in front.

Data-Based Management: Merchandising to America
from Bentonville, Arkansas

Wal-Mart's computer system houses the largest commercial or private database in the world. It is an incredible accumulation of information that is the storehouse for all Wal-Mart systems. One of the many unique uses for this extensive database is to capture 104 weeks of sales history by week for every item in every store in the world. That information can be so powerful and useful for determining merchandise sales trends, forecasting individual item sales, capturing the seasonality of many items, and managing the replenishment of each store's inventory.

It would seem to be impossible for any group of buyers to merchandise every store in the world from Bentonville, Arkansas. But this database makes it possible to accurately determine what items each store sells best and allows Wal-Mart to merchandise each store according to the specific needs of the customers who shop in that particular store. We call this the Store of the Community. Our overall objective of this program is to have the right merchandise, at the right price, in the right store, at the right time. One size does not fit all in the retail business. The computer develops a profile of the customers' merchandising needs and seasonal fluctuations that are unique to each store.

Based on local and regional profiling, the computer automatically replenishes everyday staple merchandise items in each store. But it also determines the anticipated demand on discretionary items for each store based on that store's sales history, checks the inventory of that item in that store daily, and then automatically creates an order and immediately transmits it to the nearest distribution center. The order is filled in the distribution center the next day, loaded onto a truck, and then shipped directly to the store. On a continuing basis, department managers in each store review their item movement and inventory reports and can revise the way the computer is ordering any of their items and update all the data in the system. While the replenishment of the items in each store is virtually automatic, there is always the provision for human initiative to override or refine the process.

The computer also checks the inventory of each item that is stocked in each Wal-Mart distribution center on a daily basis. Based on the anticipated demand of those items, the computer will create purchase orders and transmit them directly to the suppliers' computers overnight. On new items and strictly seasonal categories, the computer develops suggested orders for the buyers' review, based on each store's unique profile. This review is done on an exception basis. Orders are then transmitted directly to the suppliers for their shipments to our distribution centers.

This automated process has made it possible for Wal-Mart stores to be in stock consistently and minimize the dollars invested in inventory at the same time—that equals superior service for the customers and reduced capital commitment from the company. The Wal-Mart Way has always been true to our vision of satisfying our customers and maximizing the impact of our assets through excellence.

Suppliers' Access to Our Data

Our database is a crucial component of our business, and in 1991, our Information Systems Division developed a next-generation database system called Retail Link. (A more detailed explanation of the development of this unique system and the rationale for it is in chapter 9, "Reinventing the Supply Chain.") Retail Link gives our suppliers access to the Wal-Mart database in Bentonville from their own offices and on their own PCs. They can pull up any item they sell to us and monitor retail sales of that item by day, by week, by month, or by year. They have the further capability of seeing any of their items' sales by store, by district, by state, by region—or the entire company. The data is updated eight times a day, making the information current and accurate whenever they look at it. Our store associates, our buyers, and our suppliers share exactly the same data, and that makes it possible for all of us to maximize our overall performance.

The system is password-protected and has other safeguards so that each manufacturer and supplier is limited to—and protected by—studying only his or her own merchandise. Though Wal-Mart standards for merchandise sell-through are tough, we provide our suppliers with state-of-the-art feedback to

This is perhaps the most beautiful time in human history; it is really pregnant with all kinds of creative possibilities made possible by science and technology which now constitute the slave of man—if man is not enslaved by it.

—Jonas Salk

improve their product development. No one wants to create merchandise that customers don't want!

No other retailer to date has replicated this system, which is another way that technology has aided Wal-Mart in developing a significant strategic advantage in the marketplace.

Speed Matters

The Wal-Mart Information Systems Division has supported every single department in the company and is the information and communication backbone of virtually all that we do. A major point of emphasis of systems design has been to speed information to the operating divisions so that all decision-makers have accurate, timely information that they can act on.

Every morning, all store and club managers have on their desks a concise report of the status of their entire operation from the previous day, including a report card on all of their key numbers for the day and month-to-date. It also includes action steps that they need to address in that store that day. The daily report is a powerful tool to assist managers in staying informed about their business, scheduling their operations, addressing and correcting problem areas, and focusing the activities of their team each day. Managers study this report when they first come in and map out the management team's activities for the entire day. In this way they can focus in on their top priorities.

A highly respected, long-term officer in Wal-Mart's financial area shared the following incident with me recently as an example of how our investment in technology helped us to maintain our competitive advantage:

Not long ago, I was visiting with a fellow CFO about midmonth and he com-
mented that they were nearly finished closing their books for the prior month.
I asked him if they were behind schedule. He replied that they always received
their monthly financial
statements by the fif-
teenth of the following
month. I didn't have the
heart to tell him that we
had closed our books,
printed our monthly
financial reports, and

> *If something has been done a particular*
> *way for fifteen or twenty years, it's a*
> *pretty good sign, in these changing times,*
> *that it is being done the wrong way.*
> —Elliot M. Estes

had them in the hands of every manager in the chain by the third working
day of the next period. What an incredible edge over a competitor who takes
over two weeks to close the books. We have already identified our concerns,
addressed them, and moved on to bigger and better things. The competitor is
still not quite sure what to be concerned with.

This practice of immediate financial feedback and information sharing
came from Mr. Sam and was perpetuated by his great successors. In my ear-
liest days at Wal-Mart, our finance team was located just down the hall from
Sam's office on "Executive Row." We would be poring through numbers and
reviewing journals and ledgers at about 4 o'clock in the morning. Sam's old
Ford pickup would pull up outside and he would come in the door asking for
his P&L. He loved to digest reports, and had an uncanny ability to retain and
remember performances. He also expected everyone, from the CFO all the way
down to the department managers in the stores, to "know your numbers."

Technology: Friend or Foe

People in any organization can view technology as friend or foe. As much
as we have embraced change in Wal-Mart and as ingrained as change is in
our culture, it hasn't always been easy. Change is disruptive to the normal
routine and can be unsettling to those who are affected. That's another reason
why it is so important to have a culture where your people trust leadership
(and each other) and where they realize that this is all for the betterment of

the company and, in the long run, for their individual benefit as well. It is the responsibility of leadership to see that change is communicated to all associates in an effective, timely, and caring way, which will help ensure a successful implementation. All leaders must understand that we really need our people, and it is important to treat them as if we do.

Coming full circle, technology is a powerful tool in building a successful organization, but we can't accomplish anything great without the commitment of our people.

The Real Impact of Technology on Prices

In recent decades, Wal-Mart has done about as much to advance the economic life of the nation's poor people as any other institution in the nation. The nation's poor benefit greatly from access to low-priced goods. After all, the problem of poverty is the problem of not having enough money relative to the prices of needed goods. Imagine the joy of a poor single mother who can finally afford a high-quality new winter coat for a ten-year-old daughter. Imagine the poor family who can buy Christmas presents for each of their three children because twenty dollars buys three decent toys at Wal-Mart. Wal-Mart offers lower prices not because it uses factories in China (other stores use the same factories); not because it pays lower wages than other stores; but because its huge investment in information and communications technology allows it to match its wholesale purchases more carefully and quickly to consumer demand, avoiding waste and greatly lowering its costs.[2]

For reflection and action:

1. How would you rate your personal use of the various tools and resources you have available to you? Do you make things harder than they have to be?

The first rule of any technology used in a business is that automation applied to an efficient operation will magnify the efficiency. The second is that automation applied to an inefficient operation will magnify the inefficiency.
—Bill Gates

---

2. How effective do you feel your company is in the use of technology?

3. Do you feel that you've personally maximized the use of technology in your responsibility areas?

4. What are some simple, practical ways you could improve your decision making by a better approach to acquiring and processing information?

Chapter 9

Reinventing the Supply Chain

You will not find it difficult to prove that battles, campaigns, and
even wars have been won or lost primarily because of logistics.
—*General Dwight D. Eisenhower*

Wal-Mart Way Principle #9

The most basic operations in your company represent tremendous opportunities for improvement, growth, and savings. Don't overlook the obvious.

Wal-Mart grew into the largest company in the world out of one man's vision to improve the standard of living for millions of everyday people. He helped this cause by treating his team with respect and dignity—and they have always worked hard for Sam and his company. He kept the customer as his number-one priority, even passing on savings in the form of price reductions that many thought cut too deeply into margins. He built a culture of enthusiasm, hard work, and integrity. He tirelessly inspected what he expected, spending major portions of his workweek on the road and in his stores. He never stopped learning and growing. Early on, he recognized the potential of technology to support his company's vision, customers, and associates—and began a pattern of significant investment. He passed on his way of thinking and doing—the Wal-Mart Way—to a new generation of leaders who have stayed true to Sam's mandates.

Sam saw the grand picture, but he never lost sight of the details big or small. Nowhere was this more evident than in the area of logistics, which, hand in hand with Wal-Mart's use of technology, allowed the company to blow past competitors in areas of cost, real-time management of merchandise, and customer satisfaction.

Logistics is a term borrowed from the military, which refers to the acquisition and the movement of materials for the troops. It has been used in retailing for quite some time. It is basically the flow of merchandise from the manufacturer's dock to the retail counter. That sounds simple enough—so why would I put logistics on the list of major factors and core competencies impacting the success of Wal-Mart? Sure, there may be minor savings, but isn't logistics a finite process that doesn't really add top-line growth to the company's financial sheet? And doesn't every retailer have the same set of issues to deal with, which is basically moving boxes from point A to point B? How different can you really make a warehouse look and work?

In the past, retailers and manufacturers alike looked at logistics as simply a necessary evil—moving merchandise on trucks to stores. No glamour, no real opportunity or need for dramatic improvement, and certainly not an area to invest top management's time on.

But at Wal-Mart, in the same way we approached other details, we never accepted logistics as just another function to be performed in the business. We didn't accept that the way it was being done was necessarily the best way, and we believed that we could dramatically improve the entire process. Sam set a way of thinking in motion, and none of us quit challenging the traditional methods. Obviously, since everyday low prices were a major part of our customer satisfaction strategy, logistics presented a logical expense category to attack. Beyond the money-saving aspect, though, and just as importantly, we believed that this was another way to improve service to our stores and another way to separate ourselves from our competition.

Working with Suppliers to Create a Seamless Flow

One important element that all companies in the retail industry—and industry in general—had neglected was the potential of working more closely with suppliers to develop a win-win-win situation for stores, the suppliers, and the customers. By cautiously opening the door to that thinking, Wal-Mart's view of distribution and logistics expanded to include our suppliers and has become what we call the "supply chain"—a term that is now common in the industry.

Over the years, Wal-Mart has made many significant contributions to this supply-chain concept. Our logistics team has done a masterful job of improving our own internal processing and flowing of merchandise to our stores, and we have accomplished similar dynamics in creating a seamless flow between supplier and retailer through cooperation and coordination. We actually went beyond what our suppliers were doing to ship merchandise to us, examining and then making many changes to the entire relationship. In both the internal and the external arenas, the changes Wal-Mart implemented have been dramatic and the impact significant. All of their logistics developments have their own unique stories, but as they happened on parallel tracks, they are clearly intertwined.

Improving the In-House Distribution System

While many of the steps we took to improve our efficiencies within our in-house distribution system were cutting-edge and revolutionary, the overall process was gradual and evolutionary:

Phase 1: We built and operated our own warehouses to receive merchandise in order to redistribute that merchandise to our stores.

Phase 2: Next, we began to store some merchandise as a backup for our stores to order directly from our warehouses, instead of ordering from our suppliers.

Phase 3: Then we began to implement mechanization and automation, eventually converting these warehouses into full-line distribution centers complete with inventory replenishment and control systems.

Phase 4: Finally, we became a model of a vertically integrated supply chain, complete with automatic replenishment for our stores' inventories as well as comanaged inventories with many of our suppliers.

Some of these things happened almost by accident as the logistics team simply sought to fulfill the constant objective of more effectively and efficiently serving our stores so that they could, in turn, serve our customers better than any other retailer. We were open and willing to do whatever it took to make that objective a living reality. Although you will clearly see the emphasis we placed on internal efficiencies and streamlining costs in the distribution centers, it is important to understand that there were many times that we had to spend extra dollars in the distribution centers in order to save time dollars at the store level. As was the case with technology, we had to weigh tough decisions on the basis of making sure that new expenses were, in fact, investments. That consistently was the case, and this evolution of the internal functions of our supply chain further aided productivity gains in the stores and helped us reduce prices to our customers even more, in keeping with the Wal-Mart vision.

Success by Necessity

We started out by opening small warehouses and ended up reinventing the entire supply-chain concept in the retail industry. In the early years, the development of a warehouse system to receive, store, and ship merchandise to our stores was basically a necessity. Our stores were in small, rural markets, and the store managers could order only limited quantities of thousands of items of

> *Even if you are on the right track, you'll get run over if you just sit there.*
> **—Will Rogers**

merchandise. Suppliers had the expected problems in shipping so many small orders to this new and growing chain in Arkansas, and it was almost impossible to maintain a continuous flow of merchandise to our stores.

Transporting goods to our stores via big trucking companies was also problematic. The trucking companies didn't have many loads to send to our markets, so they sent the merchandise to consolidators who then held the merchandise in a warehouse until they had a large enough load to make it economical to make a delivery to the small towns and businesses in a given geographical area. In addition to costing us a premium, this system also caused major time delays and stores ran out of merchandise frequently, which was completely contrary to Sam's desire to satisfy his customers.

The First Warehouse

In order to deal with this problem, Sam leased a small building in downtown Bentonville, Arkansas, and literally became his own consolidator. Not that we were strangers to financial risk, but initially leasing the warehouse added cost to the operation without any assurance that there would be payback, which created a significant amount of worry for such a small company. Fortunately, the risk paid off in the form of greater efficiency and greater customer satisfaction, and therefore in profits.

The next step was to stock some of the staple items in the warehouse and let the store associates order these items directly from the warehouse instead of from the manufacturer. This also worked extremely well and represented

> At any point in time, there are numerous experiments under way, and many of them result in new systems that improve productivity and service. Wal-Mart culture has helped us to avoid the temptation to believe that "we have arrived." We are always acutely aware that we still have a lot more to learn.

the dawn of the Wal-Mart distribution system. We drew even closer to the full-line distribution center in 1970, when Sam built a modest headquarters in Bentonville that provided both warehouse and office space. As the company grew and more stores were added, Wal-Mart built and operated additional warehouses in the areas where the stores were being opened.

Over time, more and more of the items were added to the warehouse for convenient shipping to the stores. Eventually, over 80 percent of the merchandise that was sold in Wal-Mart stores was shipped directly from Wal-Mart warehouses. This significantly reduced the dollars tied up in inventory and improved the "in stock" position in all stores. We reached a point where we could control the flow of most of the merchandise we sold in our stores, thereby significantly improving our service to our customers. This may not sound like a big deal more than thirty years later. But remember, at that point, we were the only retailer managing freight this way, and we had established the framework for revolutionizing logistics.

Continuous Improvement

As our company grew and expanded geographically, we continued to open new warehouses. We always aimed to build in smaller communities where we could help the local economy and provide jobs for the local people—we felt a loyalty to our roots in small communities and found that the people living in these communities were usually very friendly and hardworking.

We started by looking in a general area on a map and identifying potential towns. A real-estate associate then visited all of the sites and recommended a few possibilities. We considered all the demographics involved, and then senior leadership flew out to look at the potential locations from the air— Sam liked to look at the road systems and traffic flow from that vantage— before driving around the area to take an up-close look. I remember the day that Sam and I

> *Gentlemen, the officer who doesn't know his communications and supply as well as his tactics is totally useless.*
> —General George S. Patton

flew over Cullman, Alabama, on one such trip. We had visited a number of other locations, but when Sam saw the rolling hills and chicken houses from the air he said, "Don, this is it. It looks just like northwest Arkansas."

With a keen eye to improving on past performances, we built every new warehouse with major upgrades over the previous one. Each one has been more efficient, more cost-effective, and has had greater storage capacity than the last one. In order to move more merchandise and keep up with tremendous store growth, we then developed mechanization and then automation. As these new systems and processes were implemented, the older model distribution centers were retrofitted so the entire network was kept current and uniform.

At first, we outfitted our warehouses with the usual material-handling equipment and conveyor systems that the manufacturers were producing. Over time, we began to challenge them to build equipment that was better suited to our specific needs. They ended up designing and producing equipment that no one had even envisioned, and before long, the warehouses were transformed into state-of the-art, full-line distribution centers, including conveyor systems equipped with bar-code scanners to read and sort cartons of merchandise and move those cartons from one place in the warehouse all the way to a specific point on the shipping dock and into a waiting trailer. This tremendously reduced time and costs to move merchandise. I believe that Wal-Mart was a real pioneer in the application of material-handling equipment to a retail distribution center.

> *When solving problems, dig at the roots instead of just hacking at the leaves.*
> —Anthony J. D'Angelo

I remember a time when several of our frontline associates came to me, saying they weren't able to move the merchandise through our conveyor system fast enough. We had already increased the speed of our conveyor belts as fast as they could go. Their idea was that since we couldn't safely make the belts go any faster, we needed to get our conveyor manufacturer to reduce the distance between the cartons as they moved down the conveyor and thereby improve the output. The first reaction from the manufacturer management was unyielding—they had never done it before, and they believed they couldn't do it. We encouraged them to go back to the drawing board and find a way. A few weeks later, they came back and said they could do it. They had to revise and upgrade a number of things in their camera and support systems that read the bar code. They did it for us within a short period of time.

Many of the innovations that our logistics team developed to make our distribution centers more effective and efficient are now being used in competitors' distribution centers across the country. And we've continued to make advances. In the late nineties, Wal-Mart implemented special electronic equipment, including radio-frequency-controlled order filling systems. This meant that order fillers no longer worked off of printed documents or labels. Interacting with the computer through headsets and microphones attached to control units hooked on their belts, they received voice messages to identify the location and item number of each item to be picked. They verbally replied to the computer once they pulled the item, and the computer in turn verbally verified the accuracy of the item picked. This system not only improved productivity but also improved the accuracy of the entire order filling process. In addition, we have employed a method of having the computer assign locations to inbound freight and thereby electronically controlling both the storing and retrieving of all merchandise in the building.

Not only has our use of equipment changed, but the layout of the distribution centers has continued to evolve and become more efficient. We began to build taller distribution centers so that we could use the cubic feet more effectively. In fact, we have changed just about everything we used to do in a distribution center, and we are still changing. At any point in time, there are numerous experiments under way, and many of them result in new systems that improve productivity and service. Wal-Mart culture has helped us to avoid the temptation to believe that "we have arrived." We are always acutely aware that we still have a lot more to learn.

Measuring and Tracking Performance

Over the years, the logistics team became real experts in measuring and analyzing every aspect of their operation. Just as with every other function in Wal-Mart, the team carefully scrutinized the monthly profit-and-loss statements for any slippage in performance and took corrective action immediately. Every morning, all managers in all distribution centers receive detailed recaps of the previous day's numbers for their areas. The managers then dissect each function to find areas where they can improve performance. They also continuously scan these numbers for possible systems improvements that they can make. The numbers are not just production statistics; rather, the quality of service as well as safety performance are important points of review. Wal-Mart leadership has developed incentives for outstanding performance in each area as an encouragement to the associates to excel.

Throughout the day, all distribution center managers monitor the production process on their computer screens to see how the work is flowing and where any bottlenecks may be developing. They can move associates from one area of the distribution center to another at a moment's notice in order to keep the merchandise flowing. This is incredibly important, as the staggering volume of merchandise that each center receives and ships each day makes maintaining the highest level of efficiency a crucial priority. This type of process flow analysis is quite common in manufacturing, but it has been revolutionary for distribution centers.

The Move to Food

When we decided to build Supercenters (discount stores with full-line grocery departments), we obviously needed to learn how to distribute food products. We had never done that outside of our Sam's Club bulk items, so

> *The man who can drive himself further once the effort gets painful is the man who will win.*
>
> —Roger Bannister

we began by using wholesale distributors who knew and understood the business. The canned goods and dry groceries were very similar to general merchandise, but fresh and frozen products had to be handled very differently. We had to make provisions for coolers and freezers in our distribution centers as well as for specialized trailers for shipping the merchandise to keep the products at the appropriate temperatures. After we became familiar with handling these products properly and began to move increasing volumes of food items, we decided to build our own distribution centers that specialized only in food.

As with many of the challenges we tackled at Wal-Mart, a sizable number of analysts and critics thought we wouldn't be able to efficiently distribute food. I think we actually drew energy from the naysayers—we wanted to prove them wrong again! And we did. The same evolutionary process and progress took place with food logistics as had occurred with our general merchandise distribution centers. Today we have state-of-the-art food distribution. Innovation is continuing to happen throughout the logistics network.

One Size Does Not Fit All

In the early years, deliveries were made once a week to each store. As the sales in the stores grew and we opened larger and larger stores, we had to deliver more frequently—twice a week, then every other day, and then every day for most stores. Today, many stores receive multiple deliveries every day. Each time the need arose to service the stores more effectively, the logistics systems had to be changed. The team built flexibility into every system and customized deliveries for each store, depending on size and needs. In Wal-Mart systems, we have never forced one size to fit all.

Similarly, when we first introduced Sam's Clubs, the manufacturers sent all of their shipments directly to each club. They carried a limited number of items and sold large quantities of each item. Over time, however, it became apparent that using the Wal-Mart approach would work for them as well and provide many of the same benefits for their clubs. So the systems were adapted once again, and today the Wal-Mart distribution centers handle freight for all of our retail formats: discount stores, Supercenters, Sam's Clubs, and Neighborhood Markets.

Just-in-Time Delivery: Wal-Mart Trucking

In order to control delivery to our stores on a more timely basis, we developed our own trucking operation. Instead of remaining dependent on outside carriers, who were often great but who had no obligation to take care of Wal-Mart first, it seemed natural, as we grew, to hire our own truck drivers who would become a part of the Wal-Mart team. Our trucking associates work closely with the distribution associates to make sure that we serve our stores as effectively as is possible.

Computers are a vital link in dispatching trucks to the stores and add to our efficiency in moving freight. Onboard computers are used for communications with all drivers while they are on the road. Since we already have so many outbound trucks driving down the highway and delivering merchandise to our stores, it didn't make sense to haul empty trailers back to the distribution centers on the return trip. Since we drive right by many of our suppliers' manufacturing plants, we decided to have our truckers stop and pick up that merchandise and bring it back with them, which saved significant costs on inbound freight. The onboard computers made this possible. This experiment with "back-hauling" merchandise worked, and over the years we have refined it many times. Today, our own trucks deliver over 50 percent of our inbound merchandise to our distribution centers. Again, all this may sound like the most routine of improvements. But we were the first retailer to develop a comprehensive back-haul operation. The program resulted in millions and millions of dollar savings and countless hours of savings in the movement of merchandise—all major strategic advantages.

The next step to attain even greater efficiency was to begin having our trucks pick up merchandise from a supplier for several Wal-Mart distribution centers at the same time. In order to do that, we had to develop a method we called "cross-docking." We tested the concept by building a long, narrow, extended arm on one of our new distribution centers and putting multiple doors on either side of the extension. A driver backed his truck into one of the doors on one side. As the merchandise was unloaded from that truck, some of it was moved to another truck on the opposite side bound for another distribution center. The merchandise was moved directly between trucks without any additional handling. We saved costs on shipping, handling, and many other subtle areas of our distribution system. Cross-docking became the pattern for all new distribution centers.

All of these examples reemphasize the fact that there is no limit to what we would do to improve everything in our operation.

The People Side of Trucking

Our truck drivers have always been very special associates. They are not only dedicated and hardworking, but they are also goodwill ambassadors for the company. They not only exert a positive influence on our own store associates, but they also frequently stop to help stranded motorists on the highways. I have received numerous letters from those motorists, sharing their stories and commending particular drivers for their help and pleasant manner.

One letter came from a woman who was traveling with four other women down an expressway late in the evening. She had to pull over to the shoulder of the road when a tire blew out. There they were on the side of the highway in a disabled car, in the dark. She related how fearful they were. After sitting there for a while, with many cars and trucks speeding past them, a truck finally pulled over. As soon as they saw that it was a Wal-Mart truck, they unlocked the doors and all ran and hugged the Wal-Mart driver who was then walking toward them. Her final sentence in the letter was: "Because he was with Wal-Mart we knew we could trust him." Wow! What a fantastic image of Wal-Mart—we can be trusted. We can trust our drivers to make logistics more efficient and present the smiling face of Wal-Mart at the same time.

How Can We Keep Improving?

As evidenced by the Wal-Mart distribution system and trucking operation, opportunities abound within every organization to improve operations, improve service, and reduce costs. You just have to keep looking for them. No area of a company need be stagnant—if you create an environment where your people accept that there is always a better way to do things and if you encourage and empower them to reach for higher levels of excellence. It's interesting to realize that many of the opportunities to improve are right in front of our eyes. All we have to do is be sensitive to see them and then have the courage to do something about them. Our people have had to deal with change as a way of life at Wal-Mart, but they realize that we would never have accomplished what we have without constant improvement.

Success is the sum of small efforts, repeated day in and day out.
—Robert J. Collier

The Commitment of Leadership

One area that few people truly understand about logistics is the mind-boggling array of responsibilities the senior leaders in logistics have to stay on top of due to Wal-Mart's tremendous growth. It was a balancing act to keep expenses under control while building up to twelve new one-million-square-foot distribution centers in different parts of the country and retrofitting a number of others in a single year, without letting service to the existing stores and clubs slip. And at the same time, the logistics leaders had to continue to drive innovation. No small combination of tasks!

> *Vision without a task is only a dream. A task without a vision is but drudgery. But vision with a task is a dream fulfilled.*
> —Willie Stone

When I joined Wal-Mart, it was a major struggle to get 40,000 cases a day out of a single warehouse. Today, each distribution center is consistently receiving and shipping up to 750,000 cases of merchandise a day during peak periods. Today, Wal-Mart has over 100 distribution centers with a total of 90 million square feet of space, serving discount stores, Supercenters, Sam's Clubs, and Neighborhood Markets domestically, with flexible deliveries to each store and club based on their individual needs.

Innovation has achieved millions and millions of dollars of cost savings each year, productivity continues to be improved, and processing time continues to be reduced by what has become an extensive computer-controlled network involving many of our suppliers—a system that has further reduced the cost of getting merchandise to our customers. I could go on and on about the many ways logistics has played an important role in Wal-Mart's achieving remarkable levels of success, and I used only a few of many examples to illustrate the importance of logistics. Just as technology has impacted the way many companies think and operate, so logistics has impacted the way business is conducted in the supply chain.

Our senior logistics executives have always been change-agents and have continued to adjust the way Wal-Mart handles the distribution of merchandise. They have changed systems over and over again, and the Information Systems Division became a real partner with the logistics crew. Together they have set the standard in the industry for efficient, effective distribution and continue to operate at the lowest cost of any retailer handling similar products. Logistics is clearly one of Wal-Mart's core competencies that have set us apart from our competitors.

What it takes is leadership that fosters a desire and willingness of their people to continually look for better ways to do their job, and a strong desire to be the best that they can be and work together in pursuit of that goal.

Rollin Ford, executive vice president of logistics for Wal-Mart Stores, recently shared Wal-Mart's ongoing passion in this area:

> *Reinventing the supply chain has been about much more than distribution centers, trucks and trailers, and material handling equipment. The innovations that enhanced our systems and efficiency have been remarkable, but the true impact is that it has allowed Wal-Mart to stay true to its vision of creating a great shopping experience for the average family by reducing retail prices and increasing quality merchandise options for our customers.*

For reflection and action:

1. How much attention do you pay to the most basic, ground-level aspects of your business and life? Why is it so tempting to devote time and resources to the "big" things, while ignoring the many "little" things that really add up?
2. What aspects of your business need more attention in order to improve?
3. Do you continually look for ways to improve personally? Is there any area of your life that has been off-limits to positive change? What is holding you back?
4. Take a walk through the areas of your organization where work takes place. Have a notebook and pen in hand. Can you come up with a page of areas you can improve?

Chapter 10

Creating Supplier Relationships

Coming together is the beginning.
Keeping together is progress.
Working together is success.

—Henry Ford

Wal-Mart Way Principle #10:

When you create win-win relationships with your business partnerships based on trust and open communications, you maximize your potential for growth.

Y ou can't have everyday low prices without everyday low costs. At Wal-Mart we constantly work with our suppliers to find ways to cut the costs out of our merchandise so we can pass those savings on to our customers. Effective use of technology and information systems allow us to communicate faster and more accurately with each other, and therefore, become more efficient. As pointed out in the previous chapter, the whole supply chain offers many opportunities to eliminate hidden and unnecessary costs in the handling of merchandise. But none of this is possible without cooperation and collaboration with our suppliers.

I need to tell you, it hasn't always been this way. The story of how we forged this new form of supplier-retailer partnership is every bit as vital as other keys to Wal-Mart's success.

While we were reinventing our distribution centers and other aspects of the supply chain, it was obvious that there was still a major disconnect in the system. To put it simply, we were doing our thing and suppliers were doing theirs. The relationships were basically cordial, but certainly not collaborative—we were not working together for the benefit of our customers. That had to change.

The Traditional Seller-Buyer Relationship—And a Canoe Trip

Seemingly since the beginning of time, the relationship between buyers and sellers has tended to be somewhat adversarial. The salesperson presents his or her items to a prospective buyer. They discuss a price and negotiate—the salesperson attempts to get the highest price and the buyer attempts to get the lowest price. Either they mutually agree on a price, or no sale would take place. Wal-Mart conducted business this same way in its early years. That was the common practice everyone accepted and understood.

In the late eighties, two events took place that drastically changed the entire buyer-seller dynamic between Wal-Mart and our suppliers. First, Sam Walton and a personal friend of his, a senior executive at Procter & Gamble (P&G), took their families on a canoe trip down a stream in Arkansas. In the course of conversation, they discussed the relationship between the two companies. We were one of P&G's largest customers at the time, and it was our largest supplier.

Sam told his friend that Procter & Gamble was the most difficult supplier we had to work with. His friend replied that Wal-Mart was P&G's hardest retailer to work with. They talked about what would happen if the people in the two companies worked together more closely to eliminate some of the friction. They agreed that if they could accomplish that, both companies could

> *Life is much less a competitive struggle for survival than a triumph of cooperation and creativity.*
>
> —Fritjof Capra

become much more efficient and successful and do a better job of satisfying our customers. Shortly after that canoe trip John Smale, then chairman and CEO of Procter & Gamble, called Sam and invited him and several of us to come to Cincinnati, sit down with his executive team, and see if the two companies could reach some common ground.

As a side note, this momentous meeting almost didn't happen. John Pepper, also a former CEO of P&G, shared with me an incident that occurred several days before the meeting was to take place. Sam called John

Smale and suggested that we probably couldn't make the trip because it was going to cost too much. It so happened that the hotel that P&G had reserved for us to stay in was going to cost over one hundred dollars per night, per person, and Sam said that was too expensive. (That's how serious Sam was about the corporate culture of conserving costs!) Smale said he would look into the matter and call back. Several hours later he reached Sam and said they had found another hotel and it was only going to cost fifty-nine dollars. Sam agreed we would come then. In truth, P&G had picked up the other half of the bill.

With that issue resolved, Sam and five or six of us flew to Cincinnati and spent several days reviewing the issues and discussing possible solutions. We reached a point where we all had to agree that the basic problem was a lack of trust. Fundamentally, we didn't trust them, and they didn't trust us.

The issue wasn't the integrity of either side, but the fact that the people in both companies were unwilling to share any company information with the representatives of the other company. They did things their way, we did things our way, and neither of us was even willing to consider changing. Both companies were suspicious of the other's goals and motives, carefully guarding strategies or any information that we each thought represented a competitive advantage. After all, if we told them things about our operation, they might share that information with our competitors.

We came to the conclusion that we were not really adversaries. If the people in both companies could be more open, communicate more effectively, and develop more of a trust relationship, we could have a significant positive impact on both of our businesses. Ultimately we were not competitors; we were on the same side, both wanting to sell more of our merchandise to our customers.

Dinner with Jack Welch and GE

The second event, which happened within a few months of our visit with Procter & Gamble, was a dinner meeting that Sam and several of us attended with Jack Welch and a few other General Electric (GE) executives. During dinner, we discussed how we could simplify our business relationship.

David Glass, the Wal-Mart president and CEO, suggested that an ideal picture might look like this: Wal-Mart would capture the sale by item at the

> When the board asked me to take over the bankrupt Fruit of the Loom, one of the first phone calls I received was from Wal-Mart asking me what they (Wal-Mart) could do to help.
> —Dennis Bookshester, CEO of Turtle Wax

cash register in all stores of every item GE supplied to Wal-Mart. Based on that data, the Wal-Mart computer would calculate and transmit an order for merchandise to GE over the telecommunications network on Monday directly into its computer. GE would process the order that night on its computer, fill the order on Tuesday, and ship the merchandise to us on Wednesday. We would receive the merchandise on Thursday, wire-transfer a check to GE on Friday, and reconcile any differences at the end of the quarter. We agreed that this process would require a new level of trust between the people in both of our organizations—but it was well worth a try.

Revolutionary Transformation

Today, neither of these meetings and developments sounds like a big deal. But in the late 1980s, these were revolutionary ideas. To our knowledge, no one had truly tested these waters on a large scale. As a result of these two

> Wal-Mart has always dealt with our company consistently and fairly. During the twenty-plus years that Oil-Dri has been a Wal-Mart vendor, we have found them to be among the most ethical companies with whom we do business. They have made us a better company as we have grown our systems and professionalism as they have grown. Oil-Dri is proud to be a partner with Wal-Mart.
> —Daniel Jaffee
> President and CEO of Oil-Dri

separate meetings, we eventually changed the way we transacted business with all of our suppliers. We worked closely with Procter & Gamble and GE to simplify the processes and enhance relationships, which started us on a thought process of examining everything that we had done in the past with all suppliers.

As we saw the remarkable growth and improvements that happened by working closer with Procter & Gamble and GE, we realized that once

> *Every kind of peaceful cooperation among men is primarily based on mutual trust and only secondarily on institutions such as courts of justice and police.*
> —Albert Einstein

we dealt with the issue of trust, it opened up entirely new ways of thinking and new avenues of communication. So we began exploring and talking about a partnership relationship with our suppliers, a collaboration to improve our service to the stores, to reduce costs in the supply chain, to reduce prices to our customers, and to increase sales for both the supplier and Wal-Mart.

This began an ongoing dialogue, a series of meetings between the senior leaders of Wal-Mart and our suppliers, in order to rethink and alter the nature of our relationship. Our suppliers began to see that their customers were not Wal-Mart and other retailers, but the people who bought the merchandise off our counters in the stores and clubs. Suppliers began to talk about customers as real live people, instead of "consumers." We worked together on what was good for our customers.

A beginning point in revamping our relationship with suppliers was to review and change the way we ordered merchandise, followed by a review of the entire buying process. Previously, our buyer interfaced with the supplier's salesperson, and all communication flowed between those two people. The problem was that our buyer knew our business from the all-important merchandising standpoint, but he or she did not fully understand important details about technology, logistics, accounting, or other functions in Wal-Mart. The same was true about their salespeople, which left us with continual struggles and problems in other functional areas of the company.

Our suppliers' computers were operating one way; our computers were operating in a completely different way. Their accounts-receivable department was operating under certain rules; our accounts-payable department was operating under another set of rules.

Our orders called for suppliers to ship fifteen to twenty loads of merchandise to one of our distribution centers once every two weeks, but we could unload only one of their trucks a day. We sent our orders to them on our forms and they had to reenter identical information on their forms and then into their computers. Not only did this redundancy create unnecessary work and expense, but many human mistakes were made in the translation process. The exact same thing was taking place on the invoicing side. This caused a lot of confusion and frustration at both ends.

When we were willing to sit down together and look at these processes

---

Wal-Mart and Local Suppliers

- Wal-Mart buys the vast majority of its merchandise from well over ten thousand U.S. suppliers. This includes some of the largest manufacturers in the world as well as small, even "mom and pop" suppliers, small farmers, and minority and women-owned businesses.

- Buying from these small local businesses supports Wal-Mart's Store of the Community concept, which showcases local products from local producers. For example, Wal-Mart buys apples in Washington, pumpkins in Illinois, bacon in Minnesota, pies in California, household chemicals in Colorado, barbecue sauce in Missouri, bedroom slippers in Ohio, and many other products too numerous to mention.

- Wal-Mart has established a special U.S. export office to send goods to our stores overseas. Last year, Wal-Mart sold more than $2 billion in U.S. goods in Wal-Mart stores in other countries.

with a critical eye, it was obvious that what we were doing didn't make sense. After extensive dialogue about ways to create a better, more seamless flow between us and our suppliers, our first change was to stop funneling all communications through one person at each company and find appropriate ways to get the right people talking to the right people to solve problems. We developed cross-functional teams with many of our suppliers. The teams worked together on how to simplify and streamline our communications.

Because we established a new relationship model with our suppliers, now our technology people work directly with their technology people, our logistics people work directly with their logistics people, and our accounts-payable department works directly with their accounts-receivable department. We streamlined both ordering and invoicing processes by transmitting orders and invoices electronically, directly into each other's computers, and letting the computers do the translating.

Instead of shipping fifteen or twenty truckloads every two weeks, we agreed it would be much more efficient to spread out the merchandise flow and ship just what we could handle at a given time. As a direct result of this change, we eliminated countless errors and reduced the frustration level in both companies, and we have also significantly improved the flow of merchandise through the supply chain. We have reduced inventory levels significantly and improved the "in stock" rate in our stores for our customers. Finally, we drove millions of dollars of cost out of the process for both the suppliers and Wal-Mart and have been able to reduce thousands of our prices for our customers.

Our success in establishing a trust relationship led us to develop what we described in chapter 8, a system we call Retail Link. We gave our suppliers direct access to our computers to follow and analyze on their PC screens the retail sales of all their items by store, district, region, state, or the whole country. They are now able to track daily sales on any item in any location and test new items anywhere in the country and get instant feedback on how those items are selling in the stores. We trusted that our suppliers would not share the information with our competitors, which provided a whole new foundation for our relationship with our suppliers.

No One Wins Until Everyone Wins

A fundamental element of a trust relationship that needs to be underscored is that the relationship must be beneficial for all parties involved. No one wins until everyone wins. Again, the supplier has to win, the retailer has to win, and the customer has to win—and we all won. In 1987, before we embarked on this relationship with Procter & Gamble, our annual purchases from them were approximately $350 million. In the year ending January 31, 2004, these purchases surpassed $8 billion.

Another dramatic example was what happened to the inventory turns of some items. In 1987, inventory turns on disposable diapers was approximately twenty times per year. As a result of Wal-Mart and Procter & Gamble's working together, the number of turns was increased to seventy-five times per year. This type of improvement would appear to be impossible, but it happened.

> *Our relationship with Wal-Mart is an extension of our own family. They care about us. Yes, they expect a lot of us as they do of themselves. They're wonderful at sharing direction and ideas. They will let you be as involved as you want to be, to the point of serving on some advisory boards. It's not about us or them but "we." It's a real team effort.*
> —Skip Rein, vice chairman,
> Bernstein-Rein Advertising,
> Kansas City, MO

While this is certainly an extreme case, there were thousands of items that showed marked improvement.

But the success wasn't limited to Procter & Gamble and GE. We have similar results with many, many other suppliers. In fact, the trust-relationship, open-communication revolution has impacted the entire retail industry. Retailers and suppliers all over the world have learned from what we did and changed many of their practices as well.

This is another example about striving to be the best we can be in all we do. There were obviously risks involved in what we did and investments we had to make, but everyone involved experienced enormous payback. With the changes that we instituted with our suppliers, we entered a new era of supply chain management.

Everyday Low-Cost Negotiating

Driven by our constant focus on keeping prices low for our customers, we have always attempted to buy merchandise at the lowest cost possible. The collaboration with suppliers that I have just explained has helped drive millions of dollars of unnecessary cost out of operations and logistics.

But in addition to real cost savings, I must confess that Wal-Mart buyers have always been tough negotiators. Literally hundreds and hundreds of suppliers have told me personally that Wal-Mart's buyers are the toughest negotiators in the retail industry. They are also quick to add that Wal-Mart is likewise the fairest company to work with, and that their own companies are definitely better because of doing business with Wal-Mart.

Wal-Mart leadership insists we pay our bills on time and that we keep any promises we have made to suppliers. Any buyer who accepts gifts, trips, or any other special personal considerations from a supplier will be terminated. Our buyers are rotated among departments so that their decisions remain fair and objective rather than personality-driven. Our goal has always been to keep business dealings aboveboard.

Yes, Wal-Mart can be a demanding customer for suppliers, but always in an ethical and fair manner. It stands to reason that Wal-Mart must have successful and healthy suppliers in order to stay successful itself. We depend on well over ten thousand suppliers to provide the merchandise for our stores. We need them every bit as much as they need us.

Another way that we have kept our costs down is to ask our suppliers to eliminate the practice of periodic special deals, allowances, and other forms of temporary cost reductions. How does this keep costs down? Simple. We tell them to forget the specials and sell the merchandise to us without any frills at their rock-bottom prices every day. We don't want great deals on unpopular merchandise that customers don't want unless it's drastically reduced. We believe our everyday low cost approach best serves our customers by

providing the everyday low prices and the right merchandise. It also greatly simplifies the inventory management process because we don't have to
keep track of a myriad of special deals that are still so common in the retail
industry.

Wal-Mart has also focused on working with small suppliers and minority
suppliers. It is amazing how many of these companies have experienced
rapid growth and become highly successful organizations in their own right.

> *Wal-Mart's expectations of suppliers are high but fair and their tough
> negotiation is always conducted in a professional and principled
> manner to better serve their customers. The Wal-Mart/Procter & Gamble
> partnership approach created tremendous benefits for both companies
> and changed the face of customer/supplier relationships worldwide.*
> **—Tom Muccio, retired president of**
> **Procter & Gamble Global**
> **Customer Teams and team leader of**
> **Procter & Gamble's Wal-Mart team**

We love that. Remember, Sam's original vision was to provide for customers
in small rural markets. Also, the concept of Sam's Clubs is to sell supplies
and merchandise to the owners of small businesses at lower prices than they
can get anywhere else. Although Wal-Mart has become the largest company
in the world, we are still focused on reducing the cost of living for every single
customer at every socioeconomic level. By working in partnership with our
suppliers and continuing to drive costs out, we will maintain our focus on
doing what is right for our customers.

OrangeGlo's Simple Formula for Success

How does a company go from creating, testing, refining, and manufacturing home cleaning products in the garage—using a secondhand Maytag
washer as the mixer—to grow into a major world supplier of thirty household
cleaning products with great brand recognition, including OxyClean, KaBoom,
and others? Max Appel and his wife had a simple formula that included
hard work and a dogged determination to test every sales channel.

- The Appels began selling a variety of their homegrown products at home shows and state fairs in and around Colorado in 1985.

- Through countless hours of trial and elimination, they created OrangeGlo, their first signature product. It was a squirt-and-wipe product made from orange oil, which dissolved grease, handprints, and grime from hard surfaces. After several improvements to the formula, including a better-smelling scent—derived by switching to Valencia orange oil—the product was ready for bigger markets. Max was also able to move out of his garage and into a small warehouse, where he mixed and manufactured the product.

- Max began to sell at shows away from Colorado and recruited show people to become OG distributors. At one point Max was actively marketing and selling at over one hundred consumer shows. He needed help.

- His children left successful jobs at Quaker Oats, Accenture, Young and Rubicam, and a cooking career to join their parents in building a company. Through their experience and skills, they helped to refine every aspect of the business.

- They lined up a producer and created an infomercial to demonstrate OrangeGlo and OrangeClean. The infomercial was a resounding success and helped them make the move into grocery stores such as Food Lion, Kroger, and other retail settings.

- Then came the first appointment with Wal-Mart and Sam's. Max and his son were able to convince the buyer to give the relatively unknown products a trial in some of Wal-Mart's stores, including those in Colorado where there was some previous exposure. At that time Appels' sales had reached $20 million.

- The test was a huge success at Sam's, so Wal-Mart agreed to put the Appels' products in eighteen hundred stores and eventually into the entire chain.

- Wal-Mart placed Appels' products in other countries, and the small family business was able to expand into and open corporate offices in England, Mexico, France, Germany, China, Japan, and Korea.

But what was the determining factor in the Appels' remarkable success? According to Max, it was based on a supplier relationship:

Our sales and success were due, in large part, to Wal-Mart's handling and promoting our products but even more so to their encouragement and feedback. They not only sold our products, but gave us suggestions for new products and for improving our present products. We feel blessed to be part of the Wal-Mart supply team. We feel we are partners in making helpful and unique products available to people everywhere.

For reflection and action:

1. Are there relationships in your business that could offer substantial improvements in performance if you established greater levels of communication?

2. Do you find a lack of trust between your company and business partners to be a deterrent to your success?

3. Which people in your sphere of business interactions have the most impact on your business? What potential do you see in this area?

Chapter 11

Never Stop Growing

I will go anywhere, as long as it's forward.

—*David Livingstone*

Wal-Mart Way Principle #11

The ongoing success of your organization is in direct proportion to
your ongoing commitment to grow.

What have you done for me lately? That particular phrase—common in sports and business contexts—has a strong negative connotation for most of us. It bespeaks an adversarial spirit and a lack of gratitude and appreciation for a career of significant contributions. But when we ask the question of ourselves—what have I been doing lately?—it suddenly becomes a powerful and helpful self-assessment tool to indicate the current health of an individual or company.

Growth and organizational health are inextricably linked. The Wal-Mart growth strategy has been the engine that drives the ever-expanding sales of Wal-Mart. We pushed sales relentlessly, believing that if you don't add to the top line (sales revenue), you will not be able to consistently add to the bottom line (profits). And if you don't add to the bottom line, you will not be able to reinvest in the business, which will damage every aspect of your business plan and limit your future growth.

If you've ever watched a football game on TV, you will have undoubtedly heard the phrase "they lost their momentum." It means that everything a team is trying to do is a struggle, while everything the other team is doing seems to flow so easily. During the early days of Wal-Mart's movement toward becoming the number-one retailer in the world, we caught and passed competitors who were one thousand times our size, because they didn't have an adequate growth strategy—they had lost their momentum and were heading in the wrong direction!

Sam believed in momentum. We continually plowed the lion's share of our profits straight back into the business.

The Wal-Mart growth strategy had six basic components:

1. Increase same-store and same-club sales each year.
2. Add new stores and clubs.
3. Relocate, expand, and remodel stores and clubs.
4. Acquire U.S. competitors.
5. Acquire international chains.
6. Develop new retail concepts.

Same-Store Sales

Sales increases in stores that have been open at least one year are the most important component in any company's growth plan. Why? Because if you aren't growing in existing stores, it may mean that there's a problem with your "product." Increase in same-store sales is the strongest indicator of the overall health of a retail organization. It means your merchandise and marketing strategies are still relevant. It signals that you are continuing to satisfy your customers, adding new customers, and improving your productivity at the store level. Granted, this is much simpler in growing markets, and much harder in stagnant markets. But the bottom line is, if you are unable to get increases in your existing base of stores every year, it will ultimately cause a decline in overall sales and there will be major erosion in the foundation of your business.

> *Strategy is about stretching limited resources to fit ambitious aspirations.*
> —C. K. Prahalad

A leader must keep his or her eye on the core customers and core business. I have seen many executives focus so much on new growth that they let the core business slip away. Many companies report annual sales increases on the basis of adding new stores, which allows them to hide serious flaws in their business model. By all means, an overall retail growth strategy means adding new stores, but if there's a problem with existing outlets, the astute leader will roll up his or her sleeves and start fixing things!

We recorded and analyzed same-store sales increases every single week at Wal-Mart. Those were the first numbers we looked at every Saturday morning. At the first sign of weakness, we jumped to find out what might be the problem. We didn't study the numbers for a long period of time, then establish task forces to determine possible strategies—we took corrective action immediately. In all the time I was with Wal-Mart, there never was a year when aggregate same-store sales declined.

New Stores and Clubs

The real estate department maintained a rolling five-year development plan based on target numbers and locations that it established in concert with senior leadership each year. Regional real estate managers were responsible for developing future potential sites in their market areas based on demographics and cost-effectiveness. The overall plan was to grow out from a current store base and then fill in any major gaps between stores. As soon as we developed a base of stores on the fringe of a territory, we built a new distribution center.

Our ultimate real estate strategy was to saturate a state and put stores and distribution centers as close to our customers as possible. One early tactic was to locate in a county-seat town as often as possible. We never wanted to jump to new markets too far away from our existing base of stores and extend

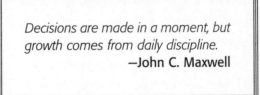

Decisions are made in a moment, but growth comes from daily discipline.
—John C. Maxwell

our logistics line too far. Bentonville, Arkansas, was actually Wal-Mart's center point, and we grew out from there in all directions.

Another important part of our strategy was to find the best possible site in a community for the best possible price. This wasn't necessarily easy—once a landowner or real estate broker heard Wal-Mart was looking at a parcel, the prices immediately spiked up. This was particularly true as we became larger and more well known.

It was important to have good visibility, enough room for adequate parking, and easy access for our customers. But there were times we had to turn down good locations because the price was too high, and we weren't willing to jeopardize everyday low prices because we paid too much for the land. We learned that lesson well with our first two Hypermarts. We overspent on both land and buildings and had to struggle to reach a profit.

Relocating, Expanding, and Remodeling Stores

We were always aggressive in relocating, expanding, and remodeling our existing stores. In many cases we simply outgrew our stores or clubs. Strong and continued same-store sales increases made it difficult to serve our customers as well as we should in certain locations—and the numbers gradually began to show that.

> *Change is inevitable, growth is intentional.*
> **—Anonymous**

If we could expand on the property we were already on, we did. If we didn't have enough room, we relocated the store or club, usually as close as we could to the existing store. I remember expanding a number of stores after being open for as short as a year-and-a-half or two years. The determining factor in deciding to relocate or expand was always whether we were serving the customers properly. When we were once again able to serve the customers better, sales went up accordingly.

Serving customers well involves maintaining a professional appearance, and after a store has been open for a number of years, it begins to look "shopworn." If a particular location didn't warrant an expansion, we went in and remodeled the store, putting in new fixtures, replacing outdated cash registers with the latest equipment—anything to freshen up the store. Whenever we did that, we experienced an almost automatic increase in sales and received great comments from our customers.

We were far more aggressive than the competition on remodeling and expanding our stores, in part because we had to be. Growing sales meant more customer traffic, which meant more wear and tear on the facility, which meant more frequent remodeling and expansion, which meant more sales . . . Whether we relocated, expanded, or remodeled a store, we never closed it for even one day. If we weren't going to let a fire shut down a store in Wabash, Indiana, for even a single week, we weren't going to let a remodel close us for even one day! We felt we owed it to our customers to remain

> *One who gains strength by overcoming obstacles possesses the only strength which can overcome adversity.*
>
> —Albert Schweitzer

open, even if the store was torn up and we were moving merchandise around. We did most of the work at night with a crew of associates from other stores and headed up by our Store Planning department.

The Acquisitions Strategy

We had many opportunities to acquire other chains over the years. We were very, very selective in choosing which ones to consider. As a result, we turned down most opportunities presented to us. The chain had to fit into our overall strategic direction and be priced right before we would become serious. One of the real advantages we looked for in these acquisitions was the quality of the people we would inherit.

Several of the acquired companies that were particularly rich in good people included Kuhns Big K, the Warehouse Club, Woolco of Canada, and ASDA of Great Britain. (I will say more on international acquisitions later.) Many of their people have risen to top ranks within Wal-Mart and continue to perform well today. It's amazing what happened when we acquired stores and continued to operate them in the same locations with almost the same type of merchandise and mostly the same people—but with Wal-Mart's everyday low-price marketing strategy and Wal-Mart's operational model. Woolco, for example, was the number-four discounter in Canada at the time we acquired it. It doubled its sales in three years and today is the runaway number-one retailer in Canada.

International Acquisitions

Selective acquisitions have been an important part of our growth, especially in the international division. When we invested in Cifra, it was already the number-one retail chain in Mexico and continues to be so today. What's even more amazing is that Cifra continues to be the fastest-growing chain percentage-wise in Mexico, not as easy a task for the largest company in a category.

ASDA was undoubtedly one of our finest acquisitions. It was already an excellent chain in Great Britain, specializing in food. The organization had great merchants and a wonderful management team from top to bottom. It was almost a perfect match with our culture; in many respects, we thought the same way and operated the same way. In fact, we were able to improve our U.S. operations by learning many things from ASDA, especially in food merchandising, while ASDA learned from us in the areas of general merchandising and systems.

Frequently when we acquired a company in another country, we found that aspects of the business infrastructure in that country were not as advanced as that of the U.S. Rather than consider this a problem or an obstacle, we viewed it as an opportunity not only to improve the performance of the acquired company, but also to assist the entire industry in order to reduce the supply-chain costs and reduce the prices to the customers in those markets. That may sound like a bold statement, but we did just that. Consider the following quote in *Newsweek:*

> When Wal-Mart strides into a new market, it's as if a bull has gotten loose in the china shop. Papers scream the news, stocks gyrate and local retailers start to scramble. Wal-Mart is already being credited with holding down inflation in Mexico, with improving Britain's cost of living and with helping to revolutionize the distribution system in China.[1]

On the other hand, several international acquisitions have been much more difficult because of cultural differences and challenges in converting

> *If you play it safe in life you've decided that you don't want to grow any more.*
>
> —Shirley Mount Hufstedler

to Wal-Mart systems. Analysts have singled out and discussed Germany, for example, for a number of years as a problem area for Wal-Mart. There is no question that it has taken us longer than anticipated to achieve the margins there we are used to. But I have never sensed negativity within Wal-Mart, rather a firm confidence that Germany will become a very profitable country for Wal-Mart in the future. We have an experienced and highly qualified leadership team in place in Germany, and it is already making it happen. As with other challenges, this has not deterred Wal-Mart from continuing to add new countries internationally, and we will continue to do so.

People who are not familiar with Wal-Mart don't understand our resolve to make things work—the greater the challenge, the greater our determination.

New Formats

The sixth component of our growth strategy has been the addition of new formats. I've already mentioned the birth of Sam's, Supercenters, international stores, and the newest format, the Neighborhood Markets. I can't tell you today what new retail concepts will emerge for Wal-Mart in the future, but I can unequivocally state: if there is a better way to serve our customers, Wal-Mart will find it.

The Wal-Mart growth strategy is the engine that drives the company's sales. Each of the six dynamics has played an important part in this continuous growth. That will be true in the future as well; however, an increasing percentage of our growth will come from the international division as we continue to bring everyday low prices and our brand of customer satisfaction to the countries we are already in and extend those values into other parts of the world.

International Wal-Mart Stores and Sam's Clubs

Country	Number of Stores*
Argentina	11
Brazil	149
Canada	248
China	43
Germany	91
South Korea	16
Mexico	694
Puerto Rico	54
United Kingdom	278

* As of January 2005

For reflection and action:

1. Does your company or organization have a growth strategy that "the troops" understand and discuss?
2. Have you encountered the temptation to expand without investing solidly in your core business base? How do you balance growth of existing assets with adding new assets?
3. What would you be willing to do to see your company grow? Write down what you believe are the four to five essential components for your organization to grow.
4. How have you handled difficulties and obstacles to growth?

Chapter 12

Good Neighbors

*Remember this: Whoever sows sparingly will also reap sparingly,
and whoever sows generously will also reap generously.*
                                      —Saint Paul (2 Corinthians 9:6)

Wal-Mart Way Principle #12

When you cultivate a spirit of charitable giving and civic involvement within
your organization, you exponentially increase your tangible and intangible
returns—including the personal character of your team.

There's much talk these days about "corporate responsibility" and what is expected of business organizations regarding their obligation to society. We never approached the subject from that standpoint—in fact, we never debated or discussed our obligation or responsibility or our failure to meet our responsibilities. Rather, Wal-Mart has been involved in its communities and all forms of charitable giving from the very beginning—because Sam wanted to. It's the way he thought. It's the way he was. It's the way our company grew. Our corporate giving is as much a part of our history and culture as anything else we do.

The Wal-Mart Philosophy of Giving

Like so many things at Wal-Mart, the company's philosophy on community giving and involvement bears the handprint of Sam Walton. Sam expected his local stores to give back to their communities through charitable giving and strongly encouraged the personal involvement of store, club, and distribution managers in local activities. He certainly practiced what he preached. He was active as a community volunteer in Bentonville, Arkansas, serving as chairman of the board of the Bentonville Chamber of Commerce and as an active member of numerous local civic organizations as well as statewide boards and personally participating in many important community issues.

He and his wife, Helen, had a particular interest in the field of education and helping young people. The family is carrying on that interest to this day through the Walton Family Foundation. Helen was a very active participant with Sam in all of their family outreach efforts. Her trademark message was that it is what you "scatter" in life, not what you "gather," that ultimately defines the life you have led. In fact, the Helen Walton Community Involvement Award is given once a year to the store, club, and distribution center that best exemplifies her philosophy through its participation with its local community.

Now, some people will read the preceding paragraphs with skepticism. The thinking is that most companies are greedy and care only about bottom-line profits; that companies do charitable acts for the free publicity that usually accompanies compassionate outreach. Why would Sam—or the company he founded—be any different? It was Saint Paul who said, "A man reaps what he sows" (Gal. 6:7). In fact, I believe the greatest return from a company's giving is not publicity, but a caring, generous workforce—and Wal-Mart has the greatest! That said, I do believe Sam had a sincere and generous heart when it came to giving, and he cultivated that personal commitment in his company.

We're talking about the Wal-Mart culture. Sam wove caring throughout our culture. Wal-Mart not only cares about Wal-Mart customers and associates, but we also care about the vitality of the communities where we serve. We want to help worthwhile organizations and needy individuals. We care deeply about the health and well-being of our communities and the people who live there. We are not casual about giving. We have a clear purpose and direction that guides all of our decisions.

Wal-Mart's style and philosophy of giving are not separate from our core business practices. Our goal has always been first and foremost to serve our customers, which is why we serve our communities, not as some faceless corporation, but as a good neighbor, and not because it's a good marketing strategy, but because it's the right thing to do.

Store of the Community

Wal-Mart wants to be a vital part of every community where we have an operating unit and help that community prosper and grow. We are not there simply to make money but to benefit that community as an active and contributing member. Store, club, and distribution

> *The service we render others is the rent we pay for our room on earth.*
> —Wilfred Grenfell

center managers are expected to be involved in their communities in a personal way by serving on the local chamber of commerce boards, civic organizations, and school boards. While we are a national organization, our charitable activities are focused on each individual store and the people we serve there.

Moreover, we believe that everyone in the company, not just managers, should be community-minded, and therefore we encourage all our associates to become involved in local organizations and volunteer their time. We even make contributions to the organizations they work with based on the number of hours they donate. As a result, each year Wal-Mart associates volunteer over one million hours (that we know about) of their personal time to local not-for-profit organizations.

To mobilize our community-building efforts, in 1979, Wal-Mart formally established the Wal-Mart Foundation. Today, the Wal-Mart Foundation has grown to be the largest corporate foundation in the nation in terms of cash giving. In fiscal year 2004, Wal-Mart Stores, Inc. contributed more than $150 million to support communities and local non-profit organizations. Customers and associates raised an additional $70 million at our stores and clubs for a total of over $220 million in contributions. The key focus areas are children's health, local education, literacy, support to our veterans, and local community support in general.

Unlike many corporate grant-making foundations, the Wal-Mart Foundation program represents a true grassroots model for charitable giving. Each store, club, and distribution center has its own budget for charitable giving, and each unit gives its money away one check at a time. Wal-Mart supports more than one hundred thousand organizations a year.

One dramatic illustration of Wal-Mart's goal that giving be local, relevant, and responsive to the specific needs of each community we serve was what Mayor Dick Murphy of San Diego, California, reported: "Wal-Mart and Sam's Club locations donated $400,000 in merchandise to San Diego County fire victims and $100,000 in cash, which went directly to the Red Cross to help support fire-relief efforts throughout San Diego County. With only two days till Halloween, local Wal-Mart associates volunteered countless hours and teamed up with the San Diego Padres to organize a Halloween party for over 400 children and their families who were victims of the fires. This type of corporate stewardship sends a positive message to the community that San Diego will persevere in this challenging time."

It wasn't the corporate home office that donated to the fire-relief efforts—it was a collection of local Wal-Marts in that area. And it wasn't some distant and exotic crisis that Wal-Mart stores wanted to help—it was the situation the communities faced where they lived.

Community Involvement Through Matching Grants

The backbone of Wal-Mart's local giving program is a matching grant program that encourages local groups to participate in their own fund-raising. We encourage them to have fund-raisers in our parking lots: bake sales, car washes, dunk tanks, car races, baseball games, and the like.

> *Everyone needs help from everyone.*
> —Bertolt Brecht

Our foundation will match the money these organizations raise at those events up to a certain level. A matching grant is a way of making sure the organizations themselves are involved in the fund-raising process, giving back to the community, taking care of the customer, and having fun in the process. Each year, a typical store will touch twenty or more organizations through this program.

We place hourly associates in charge of our charitable giving in each market, so it is not management but the hourly associates who decide by committee where donations will go: Girl Scouts, Boy Scouts, or the high-school band that needs new uniforms. We want it to be an issue of owner-ship, of making sure our

> For many years now, Wal-Mart has encouraged the Salvation Army to place their kettles outside every Wal-Mart and Sam's Club in the nation.

giving efforts stay local. Frankly, our hourly associates have a much better idea of what is important in a community than we could ever generate from the home office. When I hear some of the stories of particular outreach efforts, I am reminded of how terrific our associates are—they are caring people. They know where the real needs are in the community.

Even in the midst of all the decisions about where donations will go, it's a given that in every community that has a local United Way, that organization will have our full support. We encourage our associates to contribute to United Way through the company, and we match, dollar for dollar, the donations our associates make. During fiscal 2004, Wal-Mart contributed $19 million to the United Way in our cities and towns across America. In some towns in which we opened stores that didn't have a United Way, we were instrumental in getting one started in that community.

Each year we also give away thousands and thousands of dollars to local economic development projects in our communities, assisting in attracting other businesses to the areas as way of building and strengthening the local economies.

Just as with the company originally founded by Sam Walton, the strength of the Wal-Mart giving program is in its reliance on the local stores, clubs, and distribution centers to do what is right in their respective communities. Fortunately for many communities, this happens every day.

In recent years, Wal-Mart has developed a theme for our giving to the local communities: Good Works. If you think about it for a second, you can see that the phrase has a double or triple meaning: the projects themselves are good works; good works really do make a difference; and good people get things done!

Being a good and involved citizen has never been more important to Wal-Mart than it is today. Indeed, charitable giving has become the centerpiece of the company's legendary grand opening ceremony at every new store and club. Thousands of dollars are donated locally as part of every grand opening ceremony. Good marketing? Sure. But we truly believe it is critical for all of our new stores and clubs to get off on the right foot as a community-minded business.

> *He that will not permit his wealth to do any good for others . . . cuts himself off from the truest pleasure here and the highest happiness later.*
> —Charles Caleb Colton

A Focus on Education

One of the earliest decisions the Wal-Mart Foundation made was to annually provide a scholarship to a deserving high-school senior in each market where we had a store or club. Since 1979, the foundation has invested over $80 million in young men and women through this program. In 1995, Wal-Mart initiated a Teacher of the Year program to recognize outstanding teachers in the local school systems and make donations to their schools in their names. To date, Wal-Mart has honored more than twenty-two thousand individuals as Wal-Mart Teachers of the Year and donated more than $14 million to their respective schools.

Wal-Mart has also donated more than $16 million to the cause of literacy. Words Are Your Wheels is a program that helps nonprofit and educational groups in thousands of communities across the country that are trying to teach people young and old how to read. Wal-Mart has established a toll-free referral help line to assist individuals in locating names and telephone numbers of literacy agencies and programs. To date, nearly sixteen thousand people have received assistance through the help line.

Close Up is a charitable organization that targets underprivileged students for internships in the federal government in Washington, D.C. Mark Ramsey, an educator at the Westminster High School in Westminster, Colorado, wrote to us after receiving financial assistance from Wal-Mart for his students:

> *Because of Wal-Mart's assistance, my students have been afforded an oppor-*
> *tunity to involve themselves in learning more about our nation's history. They*
> *are empowered to become civic minded and involved. Without Wal-Mart's*
> *generous grants for low-income students, Close Up would be a program only*
> *for the privileged.*

The Environment

Wal-Mart is committed to environmental protection and preservation of our natural resources. For years, Wal-Mart has participated in environmental projects through the Wal-Mart Foundation and the many community-oriented environmental projects that our associates support. In fact, in the last five years Wal-Mart has contributed over $10 million to local environmental projects through the store grant and foundation programs.

Wal-Mart has an active environmental program at the corporate level. The goals of this environmental emphasis are:

- to ensure that our associates understand the importance that Wal-Mart places on protection of the environment as well as the conservation of natural resources;

- to be in compliance with all applicable environmental laws and regulations;

- to support local community efforts in the environmental area;

- to find new products and technologies that will minimize the environmental impact of our operations; and

- to work with our suppliers to meet the needs of the customer with products that are environmentally safe and support sustainability.

Wal-Mart is constantly exploring new technology and products when we construct, operate, maintain, and service our facilities. Some of these ideas have significant environmental impact and go well beyond compliance to environmental laws. The concept of small, experimental stores is now in its second phase with innovative ideas being built into stores and evaluated to determine if they should be included in all new stores.

Wal-Mart has an extensive recycling program within each location. In fiscal 2004, Wal-Mart recycled the following:

Corrugated Cardboard	4,413,688,000 pounds
Deposit Bottles/Cans	203,240,000 containers
Shrink-wrap	15,783,456 pounds
Tires	18,367,473 tires
Used Motor Oil	22,102,620 gallons
Used Oil Filters	16,380,011 pounds
Lead Acid Batteries	18,000,000 batteries
Disposable Cameras	36,394,436 cameras
Ink Cartridges	60,000 cartridges
Watch Batteries	6,950 pounds
Rechargeable Batteries	7,607 pounds
Silver (from photo waste)	54,147 pounds

Missing Children's Network

Not all that Wal-Mart gives back to communities is in the form of funding. Being a good citizen is much more than dollars and cents. In June 1996, Wal-Mart began a partnership with the National Center for Missing & Exploited Children (NCMEC) and created the Missing Children's Network. Bulletin boards displaying regional photos of missing children are in all Wal-Mart facilities, including more than thirty-five hundred stores, clubs, and distribution centers.

- Since the inception of the Missing Children's Network program, more than 5,864 children have been featured with more than 4,448 children found.

- So far, well over 100 of the recoveries are a direct result of a Wal-Mart customer seeing the picture of a missing child in a Wal-Mart store or Sam's Club and calling the hotline (1-800-THE-LOST) with information leading to the recovery.

- In September 1999, Wal-Mart and the NCMEC expanded the picture program to include community posters. The posters display regional photos and are distributed to local schools, libraries, and hospitals in the communities we serve.

- Local television stations air public-service announcements encouraging viewers to stop and look at the photos displayed on Wal-Mart's Missing Children Network boards.

RoadWatch

The network has been expanded to include the Wal-Mart truck drivers. The new alert is called RoadWatch—Missing Child Alert. The alert is sent directly to the cabs of our tractor-trailer units and makes our drivers aware of abducted children within their driving areas. As they go about their normal duties, they will also be watching the road for vehicles and children involved in child abduction cases.

Wal-Mart is the first company to implement this type of program and plans to share the plan and the technology with all other interested companies. Our drivers are proud to add this special RoadWatch duty to their ongoing community service actions while on our nation's roads and highways.

Code Adam Program

Another system to help children who have been abducted, Code Adam (named after the slain son of children's protection activist and television host John Walsh) became one of the largest child safety programs when it was rolled out in all Wal-Mart and Sam's Club locations in 1995. Wal-Mart associates in Crawfordville, Indiana, created the special code and it soon spread to all locations.

Code Adam is simple. When a customer shopping in one of our stores reports a missing child to a store associate, a Code Adam is announced over the public-address system. A brief description of the child is provided to all designated associates who immediately stop their normal work to search for the child and monitor all exits to prevent the child from leaving or being taken from the store.

If the child is not found within ten minutes of initiating a search, or if the child is seen accompanied by someone other than a parent or guardian, store personnel contact the local police department and request assistance.

Through a partnership with the NCMEC, the program has been shared with other companies. Currently, more than eighty Code Adam partners, including many other retailers, have implemented the program, covering more than forty-six thousand locations across the country.

In June 2003, the Code Adam Act of 2003 passed the United States Congress and mandates the implementation of the plan in all federal buildings. All of this has happened because a group of Wal-Mart associates in Crawfordville, Indiana, had the idea and made it work in their local store.

Supporting the Children's Miracle Network

Obviously, children and education are priorities with us, and while the majority of our giving is applied to local needs, we do selectively contribute to several national organizations and special causes with the goal of helping children. Since 1986, when we became involved with the Children's Miracle Network, which raises funds to enhance the equipment and services for more than 160 children's hospitals in the country, we have been that outstanding organization's largest contributor each year. We encourage our

---

The Employer for Guard and Reserve organization has presented Wal-Mart with the prestigious Corporate Patriotism Award, an honor it bestows on a company that exhibits exceptional dedication to raising awareness and support of U.S. service members and their families.

---

customers to make donations to the Children's Miracle Network in our stores, and we contribute from the Wal-Mart Foundation. We also sponsor fund-raisers for this cause throughout the year. The money we raise in each Wal-Mart location goes directly to the children's hospital closest to that location. In the eighteen years that Wal-Mart has been a contributor, we have sent over $250 million to these hospitals—over $28 million last year alone. While the checks are written to the hospitals, we look at it as though we are really giving to the needy children who are being ministered to in their time of need.

Spreading Understanding of the Free-Enterprise System

We have also been a consistent contributor to Students in Free Enterprise (SIFE). This is an organization that mobilizes students in colleges and universities across the country to develop projects both in the United States and around the globe that teach the principles of free enterprise. Since Wal-Mart is a great example of the success that can be achieved through the free-enterprise system, it seems only natural that we would be excited about an organization that does an outstanding job of encouraging and assisting students to promote this important part of our country's heritage.

When we began supporting SIFE in 1987, there were only fifteen schools involved. Now, there are more than eight hundred colleges and universities in the U.S. and another eight hundred institutions overseas, including schools in many former Communist countries. These motivated students have a better understanding of the free-enterprise system than many businessmen and women do and are having an incredible impact on the millions of people they reach every year. These SIFE students are educating children, young people, and adults alike on how the free-enterprise system functions and how it has led to the prosperity we enjoy in the United States. Professors in the schools with a SIFE program, strongly committed to the free-enterprise system themselves, are their coaches and sponsors on campus.

Annually, after regional qualifying rounds, a national and international competition takes place between the top school teams, judged by the senior executives of some of the largest and most successful companies in the country. Having been a judge for a number of years, I myself can say that they are some of the brightest young people in our country and will be future leaders in our society. Wal-Mart, as numerous other companies have done, has recruited many of these students to become Wal-Mart associates. Many have advanced in the company and have been identified as high-potential leaders in Wal-Mart.

Patriotic Commitment

Another example of the impact that local stores and clubs are capable of is what we did in connection with the new World War II Memorial in Washington, D.C. In 2001, the local stores, clubs, and distribution centers raised $8.5 million through various activities with our customers, adding to the $6 million contribution made directly by Wal-Mart Stores, Inc. The WWII memorial opened Memorial Day Weekend 2004, and the company was represented at the ceremony not by our CEO, but by twenty WWII veterans who work for Wal-Mart today. Wal-Mart also undertook a similar effort to support the reopening of the Statue of Liberty, which had been closed since September 11, 2001.

We don't do this for publicity—we do it because we want to and because we believe that it is the right thing to do. We have never wanted to toot our own horn. We don't ever want our communities or our own people to get the idea that the reason we give back to communities is to pat ourselves on the back. And even when we try to encourage our associates to ask the local newspaper to come out and take pictures of various events, we do it so that people in the community will better appreciate the Boy Scouts, the Boys and Girls Club, organizations that help with handicapped kids, or whoever it is we are helping to support and promote a cause. We strive to gain greater exposure for the organizations in order to encourage others to give to them as well.

Giving in Other Countries

As we have moved into other countries, the Wal-Mart community involvement philosophy has been an important part of the culture transfer that has taken place in each country. Basically, the stores have followed the exact same philosophy as that in the United States, although they may implement them differently in each country. As in our U.S. stores, it's up to the associates in each individual store to come up with the ideas of how to give and whom to give to. Associates in stores outside the U.S. are every bit as involved as the associates in our U.S. stores. Their ideas are always innovative, and there are many stories about how they have acted as good neighbors in their own countries.

One interesting story comes from Germany, where tremendous flooding occurred in 2002. The associates in one of the towns that was hit hardest invited hundreds of the townspeople who were driven from their homes to spend a number of nights sleeping on the floor in the Wal-Mart store. They also set up tents in the parking lot and tried to create as comfortable sleeping arrangements as they could. The German people perceived this as a wonderful act of compassion by Wal-Mart, but it was also a great boost to the morale of the associates in the store. One of them shared with me how proud they all were to be a part of a company that cared so much about helping people who were in need. Our executives in the International Division have made community involvement a priority in the strategic development of each new country, demonstrating to the world that we care about people everywhere.

The leadership team at Wal-Mart has always believed in being contributing members of our communities. Sam expected it. The result has been a substantial and comprehensive program that touches the lives of people every day. While the primary focus has been on making significant, matching-dollar contributions each year that go to specific local priorities, it has mushroomed far beyond that, encompassing major national and international efforts to promote the free-enterprise system around the world, to relieve suffering in

---

Each man should give what he has decided in his heart to give, not reluctantly or under compulsion, for God loves a cheerful giver.
—Saint Paul (2 Corinthians 9:7)

---

children's hospitals, to build and restore national monuments, to assist in literacy projects and many other education initiatives, to develop relevant nonfinancial programs that help to protect our youth and children, and to systematically encourage our own associates to volunteer their time to worthwhile not-for-profit organizations.

Since most of our giving has been local in nature, many people are unaware of the size and impact our program has had. In many of our large market cities, programs such as Good Works seem to go unnoticed—unless there is a major disaster. That's the way it should be. Our deepest satisfaction comes from knowing we are doing the right thing—and the appreciation we have received from those thousands and thousands of individuals and organizations whom Wal-Mart giving has directly impacted.

> *At a time when it was needed the most, Wal-Mart has extended its hand to support a 104-year old tradition that benefits many thousands of people in communities throughout the United States, "Every dollar put into our Red Kettles is used locally, and Wal-Mart's generosity by matching those dollars will extend our local services to many more needy individuals requiring our assistance far beyond the holiday season."*
>
> **—Commissioner W. Todd Bassett,**
> **National Commander of The Salvation Army**

Wal-Mart Giving At-a-Glance

- In 2003, *Forbes* magazine recognized Wal-Mart Stores, Inc. as the Largest Corporate Cash Giver. The magazine cited *The Chronicle of Philanthropy's* annual survey based on sales and cash donations.

- Last year, Wal-Mart, Sam's Clubs, and distribution centers provided grants to more than one hundred thousand local nonprofit organizations to help address causes that matter most in their communities.

- Wal-Mart supports many organizations and events that represent the ethnic diversity of our associates, customers, and communities both nationally and at the local level. Partnerships include the

National Association for the Advancement of Colored People
(NAACP), Congressional Black Caucus, the Congressional Hispanic
Caucus, National Council of La Raza, Mexican American Legal
Defense and Education Fund, United Negro College Fund, as well as
other community-based organizations committed to improving the
quality of life for all members of our communities.

For reflection and action:

1. Does your company—do you—consider giving important? Why or
   why not?
2. Has anyone ever helped you at a time when you needed it? What did
   that teach you about service and need?
3. Are there any issues that are particularly important to you and your
   company—any people you feel particularly passionate about helping?
   What would it take to mobilize your organization to get involved?
4. What can you personally do for someone today? What can you do to
   move your company toward a more compassionate attitude?

Scaling New Heights:
The Future for Wal-Mart

This thing we've got going with our company and our people is
so gratifying to me that I find it very easy to be enthusiastic
about our future and to be optimistic about what we can
accomplish together.

—**Sam Walton**

E arly in 2002, the official announcement was made from Bentonville, Arkansas: Wal-Mart was now recognized as the largest company in the world. It was greeted with great fanfare—and I'm sure just a little incredulity—by the media worldwide. Even though I knew we were close to achieving that milestone, and the press release came as no real surprise, I was still utterly amazed. What a journey! We had scaled the heights of the corporate world, and now we could stop for a moment and survey the magnificent view. Or could we?

Recently as I thought about what's next for Wal-Mart, I was pleased—and challenged—to read the following editorial comment by *Good to Great* author, Jim Collins, in *Fast Company* magazine, which I thought powerfully captured the "state of the union" for Wal-Mart:

> *If current growth rates hold up, the company that Sam Walton built will*
> *become the world's first trillion dollar business within a decade. Far fetched?*
> *Perhaps. It is entirely possible for a company to grow to 1.4 million people and*
> *retain much of the vibrant culture and sense of purpose created by its entre-*
> *preneurial founder. I must admit, I hadn't thought it was possible. By the*
> *time most companies reach $10 or $20 billion in revenue, they have long ago*
> *lost the entrepreneurial zeal that fueled them in the first place. By $50 billion,*
> *they have gone fully corporate, and their very success has made them compla-*
> *cent, dull, and slow. The usual story is what was once a fast company—in its*

attitude, its values, its spirit, its execution—eventually succumbs to inertia and
spirals into a doom loop of mediocrity. Yet if anything, Wal-Mart is gaining
momentum.[1]

I was reminded that even if we had scaled a mighty mountain, now was no time for Wal-Mart to rest on its laurels and enjoy the scenery. Why? I believe that some of the very the best chapters in the Wal-Mart story are not yet written—but are to come in the days ahead. Wal-Mart truly is gaining momentum. It will continue to grow at a powerful pace for the foreseeable future. The story is not finished. It's true—there are more mountains to climb.

Consider that Wal-Mart's aggressive growth and capital investment strategy for fiscal year 2005 includes adding 320 to 345 new stores in the United States alone. The company will add more than 50 million square feet of new retail space, an increase of more than 8 percent. The growth rate for new stores and retail space in the international arena will be much greater.

I believe the future has never looked brighter for Wal-Mart than today. But that success will only be achieved . . .

- as long as the leadership and associates remain true to the vision that Sam had of serving others.

- as long as we don't let our success go to our heads and believe that we are invincible, that success will just magically continue as we float along effortlessly, or that we are somehow entitled to success.

- as long as we don't become arrogant and let our egos get in the way of the job that needs to be done.

- as long as we continue to treat everyone with respect and dignity, no matter what their title or position may be.

- as long as we remember that we are family and that it takes all of us to succeed.

- as long as we never betray our values and continue to uphold them, no matter what it costs in short-term sales or profits.

- as long as we fight to keep our unique culture alive every hour of every day.

- as long as we remember that the only one "boss" in Wal-Mart is the customer—every single one of them—and that they are the reason we are in business.

- as long as we continue to provide value to those customers by offering quality merchandise at everyday low prices.

- as long as we don't focus on the weaknesses of others—but on continually improving ourselves.

- as long as we continue to look for large and small ways to improve our operations and logistics, while driving out unnecessary costs.

I know that such bold talk may turn some people off because it sounds too simple, perhaps a little trite, and for sure quite arrogant. (Of course, I don't think Sir Edmund Hillary would have reached the summit of Mt. Everest were it not for bit of boldness.) I confess that I like to keep things simple, and I never want to be trite or arrogant. But I feel justified in being so straightforward in these closing pages because the Wal-Mart record stands for itself. Others could have done what Wal-Mart did—and tried. *But only Wal-Mart became and is Wal-Mart.*

I'm proud of the opportunity I had to be a part of one of the greatest business stories ever told. I am thankful every day to Sam Walton, who trusted me and gave me that opportunity.

And now my hope for you is that in at least a few small ways (and perhaps on a deep and profound level) your heart, mind, and soul will be inspired by *The Wal-Mart Way* and that it will show you some new ways to make your organization more vital—and to help you to grow as a person and build on your own dreams.

Wherever you are on your journey, whatever mountain you must climb to reach your destination, know that you can get there . . .

- as long as you have a vision to help others.

- as long as you stay true to that vision and treat others with dignity and respect.

- as long as you provide more than your customers expect, work with excellence, stay humble, and always look for ways to do things better.

- as long as you share your blessings with others.

If you follow those principles, you just might discover that even greater opportunities and tasks await you. In the words of former U.N. General Secretary Dag Hammarskjöld:

> *Never measure the height of a mountain, until you have reached the top. Then you will see how low it was.*

May God bless you on your way!

About the Author

Don Soderquist joined Wal-Mart Stores, Inc., in 1980 where he served as executive vice president, vice chairman and chief operating officer, and finally senior vice chairman. Continuing Sam Walton's legacy, he became known as the "keeper of the culture." As CEO, Don led Wal-Mart during a period of exponential growth as it grew from the largest retailer in the world to the largest company in the world.

Don received his B.A. degree in Business Administration from Wheaton College in Illinois. In 1996, Don was inducted into the Retailing Hall of Fame, and in 1998, John Brown University created the Soderquist Center for Business Leadership and Ethics in his honor.

Acknowledgments

There are many people who have provided support and encouragement in the writing of this book. It would be impossible to include the names of all of them because my story really began in April, 1980, when I responded to Sam Walton's invitation to move my family to Bentonville, Arkansas, and join this relatively small discount store chain. Over the years there were literally thousands of Wal-Mart associates and supplier representatives who played an important part in my understanding of the principles I have attempted to share with you. In the beginning, I thought that the success was as a result of what we did. After being with the company for a few years, it became apparent that it was really because of what we believed and how that was reflected in our culture.

After I retired from Wal-Mart, Ken Blanchard, the author of many books including *The One Minute Manager*®, became a constant encourager to share my view of the magic behind the success of Wal-Mart. He even spent personal time with me sharing his thoughts about my approach to writing the book. My wife, Jo, and our children and their spouses also believed that my perspective could be helpful to present and future leaders in all fields of endeavor. I am also grateful to a number of friends I have known along the way—who also know Wal-Mart—who honored me by providing quotes and endorsements.

Mark Gilroy, a gifted writer, was extremely helpful in taking my manuscript in rough form and challenging my organization and structure, smoothing the transitions, clarifying my thoughts and words, and articulating the principles.

I am thankful for my team at Thomas Nelson: the encouragement from Jonathan Merkh and the editing talents of Brian Hampton and Kyle Olund (along with a little last-minute help from Kristen Lucas).

Many, many Wal-Mart associates and executives who reminded me of the details of their special experiences including Lois Richard, Pete Maldanado, Del Sloneker, Sam Dunn, and Harry Jordan. Numerous Wal-

Mart suppliers with particular help from Max Appel on his wonderful story of entrepreneurship.

I greatly appreciate the research assistance, as well as careful scrutiny of the facts, by Rex Horner, Jay Allen, Bob Connolly, Rick Tuel, Fred Disch, and Tom Hyde from Wal-Mart; retired Wal-Mart executive Paul Higham, and John Spenst of the Soderquist Center for Leadership and Ethics.

Finally, for their assistance in clerical and detail follow-up I appreciate my assistant, Pat McKee, as well as Beverly Turrentine, Sarah Clark, Jennifer Harris-Frowen, Julie Mitchell, Dawn Hollabaugh, Andy Wilson, and all the associates at the Soderquist Center for Leadership and Ethics.

The Wal-Mart Way Principles

Wal-Mart Way Principle # 1
Every successful venture begins with a dream that requires determination, passion, and the willingness to grow if it is to be fulfilled.

Wal-Mart Way Principle #2
You must have a vision that allows you to see a bigger, better, stronger you in the future—while never taking your eyes off of who you are and what you are doing today.

Wal-Mart Way Principle #3
To build a great company, you must create a culture where everyone shares the same values, purposes, and expectations of success.

Wal-Mart Way Principle #4
True success is achieved in direct proportion to the degree that an organization treats its people with respect and dignity—and believes in them enough to help them grow.

Wal-Mart Way Principle #5
You will succeed when you make a commitment to help your customers succeed first.

Wal-Mart Way Principle #6
Achieving excellence becomes a reality when you set high expectations, humbly face and correct your mistakes, stay optimistic, and avoid the quicksand of complacency.

Wal-Mart Way Principle #7
Your success is in direct proportion to your ability to plan, monitor, and ultimately execute all phases of your business.

Wal-Mart Way Principle #8

To build a great company, you must actively and continually seek out, evaluate, and invest in the tools that best serve the people and aims of your organization.

Wal-Mart Way Principle #9

The most basic operations in your company represent tremendous opportunities for improvement, growth, and savings. Don't overlook the obvious.

Wal-Mart Way Principle #10

When you create win-win relationships with your business partnerships based on trust and open communications, you maximize your potential for growth.

Wal-Mart Way Principle #11

The ongoing success of your organization is in direct proportion to your ongoing commitment to grow.

Wal-Mart Way Principle #12

When you cultivate a spirit of charitable giving and civic involvement within your organization, you exponentially increase your tangible and intangible returns—including the personal character of your team.

Perspective on External Criticism of Wal-Mart

As Wal-Mart has grown to become the largest company in the world, so too has the public focus on the company. Today, Wal-Mart is very likely the most visible and scrutinized company in the United States. Because of the company's size and success, it has become a lightning rod for some of the most challenging issues we face as a society and country. Wal-Mart is featured prominently in the public debates on health care, world trade, revitalization of downtown areas, and even the free enterprise system itself. Moreover, now the company finds itself in a position where it is judged on a standard of perfection. Every mistake has the potential to appear on the evening news or on the front page of the local newspaper. To put it another way, with more than one million people working for Wal-Mart in the U.S., the company has become larger than many big cities. Can you imagine a city of one million people, for example, that is held to a standard of zero mistakes by its citizens?

In addition, like any successful company or organization, the company faces challenges from a host of detractors who want to slow or completely stop the company's growth. In recent years, many of these have chosen to attack Wal-Mart's reputation rather than trying to compete with the company at the retail level. These reputation attacks can take the form of lawsuits, negative coverage in the news media, laws and regulations written specifically with Wal-Mart in mind, and even organizing activity by labor unions in the company's stores.

All this said, Wal-Mart leaders are the first to say the company is not perfect and needs to improve. This commitment to "continual improvement" was a personal priority for Sam Walton, and it remains an important part of the Wal-Mart culture today. Ironically, those who attack Wal-Mart will ultimately play a key role in making it a better company, and even a more successful retailer.

Recommended Reading

GOOD TO GREAT
Why Some Companies Make the Leap . . . and Others Don't
by Jim Collins

SOUL OF THE FIRM
by C. William Pollard

LEADERSHIP BY THE BOOK
Tools to Transform Your Workplace
by Ken Blanchard, Bill Hybels, and Phil Hodges

PRIMAL LEADERSHIP
Realizing the Power of Emotional Intelligence
by Daniel Goleman, Annie McKee, and Richard E. Boyatzis

LEADING CHANGE
by John P. Kotter

IF ARISTOTLE RAN GENERAL MOTORS
The New Soul of Business
by Thomas V. Morris

CREDIBILITY
How Leaders Gain and Lose It, Why People Demand It
by James M. Kouzes and Barry Z. Posner

THE LEADERSHIP ENGINE
How Winning Companies Build Leaders at Every Level
by Noel M. Tichy with Eli Cohen

THE FIVE TEMPTATIONS OF A CEO
A Leadership Fable
by Patrick M. Lencioni

AUTHENTIC LEADERSHIP
Rediscovering the Secrets to Creating Lasting Value
by Bill George

Notes

Chapter 7

1. Constance L. Hays, "The Wal-Mart Way Becomes Topic A in Business Schools," *New York Times*, July 27, 2003.

2. Bradford C. Johnson, "Retail: The Wal-Mart Effect," *The McKinsey Quarterly*, 2002, No. 1.

Chapter 8

1. Johnson, "Retail: The Wal-Mart Effect."

2. Steve Berry, James Burrows Moffat, professors of economics, "Wal-Mart Is No Enemy—It's a Boon for the City's Shoppers," Yale University's *Daily News*, January 16, 2003.

Chapter 11

1. Richard Ernsberger Jr., "Wal-Mart World," *Newsweek*, May 20, 2002.

Conclusion

1. Jim Collins, "Bigger, Better, Faster," *Fast Company*, June 2003, page 74.

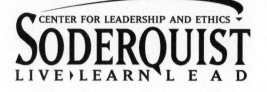

CENTER FOR LEADERSHIP AND ETHICS ▼

SODERQUIST
LIVE›LEARN L E A D

Founded in 1998, the **Soderquist Center for Leadership and Ethics** is a not-for-profit organization located in Siloam Springs, Arkansas, and affiliated with John Brown University. The Center is named for Don Soderquist, who firmly believes that business ethics are not a luxury, but an essential element in creating a high-performance organization; he also understands that the responsibility for creating an ethical organization belongs to its senior leaders. The Center, which exists to equip men and women with the transforming power of ethical leadership, hosts retreats at its retreat center located on the shores of beautiful Beaver Lake in Northwest Arkansas for CEOs and other senior leaders to dialogue with their peers and explore how to become more effective and successful principled-centered leaders. In addition, retreats are held for high-potential and fast-track middle managers and senior leaders to significantly accelerate their development. By creating, developing, and implementing customized strategic planning, succession planning, strategic alignment sessions, and leadership development paths for organizations, their leaders, and their people, the Soderquist Center has become a catalyst for organizations that want to move from today's reality to the unlimited possibilities of the future.

We invite you to explore our Web site:

www.soderquist.org

If you enjoyed *The Wal-Mart Way* by Don Soderquist, consider these other quality leadership titles from Nelson Business:

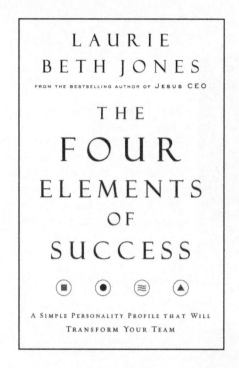

LAURIE
BETH JONES

FROM THE BESTSELLING AUTHOR OF JESUS CEO

THE

FOUR

ELEMENTS

OF

SUCCESS

A SIMPLE PERSONALITY PROFILE THAT WILL
TRANSFORM YOUR TEAM

THE FOUR ELEMENTS OF SUCCESS

Small businesses, large corporations, churches, and organizations of all sizes need to have an easily understood method for hiring, placement, team building, and personnel integration so that all members in the organizational ladder can be at their effective best. *New York Times* best-selling author Laurie Beth Jones developed the Path Elements Profile (PEP), which can be used in recruitment, placement, retention, team building, and customer relations. Based upon the elements of Earth, Water, Wind, and Fire, *The Four Elements of Success* will help leaders determine both individual and team behavioral tendencies that affect everything. INCLUDES an assessment test for your team's elemental strengths and weaknesses.

ISBN: 0-7852-0888-7

NELSON BUSINESS
A Division of Thomas Nelson Publishers
Since 1798

More titles from Nelson Business:

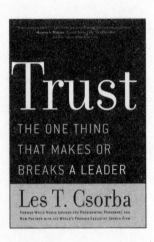

TRUST

From the perspective of someone who served a U.S. president, a U.S. senator, and a governor, author Les T. Csorba sees trust as the most indispensable force between leaders and followers. In *Trust* he offers observations gleaned from two decades of experience in government, business, church, and family. The book features interactive elements such as a guide to evaluating whether you are developing the trust necessary to motivate and richly lead followers.

ISBN 0-7852-6154-0

AESOP & THE CEO

David Noonan, in a clever melding of modern business sense and ancient wisdom, uses the ancient fables of Aesop as a backdrop for 50 significant lessons from the greatest business leaders of our day. Both entertaining and informative, *Aesop & the CEO* is comprised of short, easy-to-read vignettes that cover every aspect of corporate life: negotiations, hiring and firing, mergers and acquisitions, marketing and sales, and day-to-day management.

ISBN 0-7852-6010-2

NELSON BUSINESS
A Division of Thomas Nelson Publishers
Since 1798